## Praise for *Souvenirs of the Holy*

"Like a child opening a treasure box filled with cherished trinkets, collected rocks, and precious memories, Brock invites us to see(k) the extraordinary in the ordinary. *Souvenirs of the Holy* is a thoughtful and honest gift from a wise traveler, treasure hunter, and friend, generously shared with anyone seeking the sacredness in life's everyday moments and the boundless treasures that love brings."

—**Roger Hutchison,** author of *The Gift of Baptism*, artist, and Christian educator

"A cast iron skillet in a kitchen, a rock along a stream, a scar on a body: These everyday objects infuse our ordinary lives with divine simplicity, connecting people to places in a sacred world. Through accessible words and meditations, Laurie Brock reminds us to connect with the everyday as a form of contemplation and grounding but also as a pathway to our collective power in a world more overwhelming than calming. After reading *Souvenirs of the Holy*, I feel less fearful of our uncertain future and more equipped to draw on the energy of the sacred in my household, my community, and beyond."

—**Mallory McDuff**, PhD, author of *Our Last Best Act* and *Love Your Mother*

"This is a book not about our shiniest, most prized possessions but about the everyday, oft-overlooked items that mean the most. Laurie Brock's writing has me not only imagining a meal from her grandmother's seasoned cast iron skillet, but wanting to share the story of my own inherited belongings that remind me of my 'belonging.' She beautifully weaves together the stories of our hearts with the good news that we are small but beautiful fabric scraps in God's incredible tapestry."

—**Callie Swanlund**, priest and author of *From Weary to Wholehearted*

# Souvenirs of the Holy

LAURIE M. BROCK

# Souvenirs of the Holy

*Encountering God Through Everyday Objects*

Broadleaf Books
Minneapolis

SOUVENIRS OF THE HOLY
Encountering God Through Everyday Objects



31 30 29 28 27 26 25 1 2 3 4 5 6 7 8 9



Library of Congress Control Number: 2025932564 (print)

Cover design by Amanda Kain
Cover image © 2025 Getty Images; Grungy Cast Iron Skillet/93057851 by busypix

Print ISBN: 979-8-8898-3195-2

eBook ISBN: 979-8-8898-3196-9

Printed in China

*To my sister, Nikki, for being part of so many conversations about our family's weird and unhealthy relationship with stuff. Over the years, the words settled into small spaces and created the foundation for this book. Things are always things, and they are also rarely just things.*

# CONTENTS

# INTRODUCTION

THE MONASTERY NEAR my home is quite sparse. The rooms for retreatants at the Abbey of Gethsemani are simple—a bed, a chair, maybe a desk, almost always a cross on the wall, and maybe an icon of a saint. The interior of the church itself, redone in the past century, is meager too, with uniform pews, white walls, dark beams, and a cross and altar. No stained glass. No lavish adornments. Just a space with a minimum number of things.

I often slide off to the monastery for a few hours when the world becomes too much, when I have not tended well to myself. I'm an Episcopal priest, and like everyone else, sometimes I get overwhelmed by all the noise and need of the world. So I go to a place of quiet filled with space and sparseness. There, like so many wanderers and pilgrims and faithful and even faithless before me, I find solace in monastic simplicity, even bareness.

The holiness of monasteries resonates with many of us because of the lack of things. Monasteries are often furnished sparingly and functionally. For those of us who drop in to visit, the spare décor is a welcomed change from to-do lists and claims on our time. The sparseness reminds us to strip down to the minimum of faith. The abundance of uncluttered space invites us to wonder about what we actually need.

What, in fact, do we actually need, both in the material world and in the world of the Spirit, as we live and move and have our being? What is essential? What is extraneous? What do we *think* we need, and what do we truly need?

Vows of poverty mean that items owned by monastic communities are very few and usually serve a function: pots to cook with, chairs to invite us to sit, and curtains to shield us from the sunlight. But I've been in enough monasteries and spiritual retreat centers and churches to know the things in those places don't always serve a utilitarian purpose. Many things in these holy spaces are simply beautiful, with no clear function except to bid us to touch something beautiful: icons on bare walls, statues in the middle of a woodland, a vase of fresh flowers on a side table.

The Brothers of Gethsemani are a functional bunch, although not entirely. Scattered about the monastery and its grounds are things that aren't purely functional. Statues, some small, some larger, mark places of prayer around the grounds, welcoming visitors to touch something of God in the marble, metal, and stone. There are flower gardens, cultivated yet rampant with splendor.

Then there is the graveyard. Gethsemani's graveyard is less ornate than many cemeteries, yet one grave in particular is anything but sparse. As I sat in the graveyard during one visit, I watched a young man—who might have been in his mid-twenties but looked like he could barely drive legally—hang a rosary on one specific marker for the grave. The grave was already draped with rosaries, and flowers, from fresh to fading, surrounded the simple cross that marked the grave.

I've been to Gethsemani enough to know that the other monks don't remove the tokens left on this particular grave for Brother Louis. His non-monastic name was Thomas Merton, and he was a famous monk who expanded and challenged many restrained ideas of God and holiness. People come to this place because of Thomas Merton's words and his legacy, and they often want to leave a part of themselves here in thanksgiving and homage.

The many things that adorn Merton's grave speak of prayers that people long to solidify into a tangible piece of matter. In this place of bareness, of vows of poverty, of minimalism, things still slip in: physical souvenirs of the holy.

Sometimes prayers, memories, and emotions are so valuable, so pressing, that they need to take up space.

We humans need things. We need items, objects, and belongings that we can grasp and touch and grab and even fearfully hold to remind us. We need reminders that we are here and that God is here. Things are always things, and they are also rarely just things.

Granted, we often have a difficult time finding a balance between *none* of the things and *all* of the things. Many of us wax and wane between the two extremes. For a while we follow gurus and self-help books that tell us to buy all the things—because life is short, and we only live once, and really we just can't live without the latest smartphone or the newest fall fashion or the most updated accent lamps for our end tables. Then, eighteen months to two years later, we hear another guru or consultant or best-selling author tell us we need to get *rid* of all the things—because minimalism is what it takes to be truly happy.

As with many things in life, the truth is likely somewhere in the middle. Most of us would do well to have fewer things, but perhaps we'd be better off investing *more* meaning, rather than less, in those items.

Because some things are *more* than things, aren't they? They hold something of our feelings, our hopes and expectations, our grief and remembrances, even our faith. A luxury of rosaries on Thomas Merton's grave isn't draped there only for decoration. The rosaries are there because they represent something that needs to be touched, held, expressed, and seen, something more than an ephemeral idea spoken into the world.

Yes, the emotions, mystery, and indefinable parts of our existence are just as real as the things we touch and hold. But sometimes we need tangible, substantial parts of this vast creation to represent the things we cannot touch.

I doubt too many of us have a spiritual attachment to our vacuums. Yet we also possess things that are souvenirs of the holy. A rock we picked up may give us a way to touch again the moment on a walk in our neighborhood when we witnessed a sunset that moved us to silent awe. A book, an item of clothing, a dried flower from a hike are all souvenirs, things that represent moments and emotions that can't easily be expressed and desperately need to be incarnate in some form. Things can serve as memory holders for times of our lives that we are fearful of forgetting—or even for things we'd sooner forget. Perhaps something wise in our souls knows we will benefit from that memory at some point, so we hold on to the thing that reminds us of pain, or suffering, or grief.

From quiet gratitude to despair, from joy to awe, we humans allow things to function as mediators: conduits of our memories, our feelings, and even our relationship with God. Things tell stories about us, and stories about what we find holy. A walk through our homes will likely nudge us to recall all sorts of emotions and events. Items speak the stories of our lives, if we let them. And the stories of our lives are holy.

Things, like faith, can shift. We may treasure some things for a lifetime; other things we may decide to give away when our souls no longer need them. Our things will remain long after we have returned to ashes and dust. Seeing objects as souvenirs of the holy may help us share our reckless and cautious life of faith. Walking through the spaces we inhabit, do we let things tell the stories of our encounters with God? Have we shared the power of these objects with those we love so they know the stories?

Things speak of our story. They are souvenirs of our holy journeys. Treasure them. Listen to the truths they whisper. Hold them until the time comes to release them to serve another.

I invite you to join me in this reflection on fifteen types of items that connect us to God, to memory, and to the seam of stories running underneath the tangible world. Each chapter focuses on particular things in my life—such as cast iron, scars, garden shears, and reins—that speak to me of the Spirit in some way.

As you read, you may find yourself latching on to the specific thing I describe in the chapter—your own calendar, your own shoes, a rock you hold dear, the quilt on your bed—and letting that thing in your life speak to you. Then again, the fifteen things in this book are particular to who I am and the life I live as a white woman who is a writer and priest and equestrian shaped by her life in the South. Your souvenirs of the holy might be very different from mine. In that case, let the thing in each chapter lead you toward deeper reflection on whatever it is in your life that connects you to God and the spiritual life. What in *your* life speaks of survival? Of vulnerability? Of melancholy? Of usefulness? Of meandering?

In these pages, I let things and their stories, their forms, their tangibility, and their sacredness speak. If we listen carefully, our things may preach a kind of sermon, reminding us of the truths we know. Things may offer a kind of spiritual direction, helping us determine the movement of God in the world. They may hold a kind of wisdom, showing us the way. At the end of the book are four prayers and meditations that invite you to find objects in your own life, in your own space, and listen to the sermon they might preach to you.

God speaks to us through so much, and too often we are so busy that we miss the words of love, the emotions that lead us to excavate more deeply in our souls, and the many ways

God asks us to listen, to learn, to live this adventure of faith. We don't always need to go to a monastery or a church or some other designated sacred space to hear and feel God with us. Sometimes we just need to look around at the things, the objects, the souvenirs of the holy already present, just waiting for us to listen. They are relics and touchstones and items that remind us of the people we've known, the places we've seen, and the love we've experienced. All these are mementos of the ways we've encountered God. They are waiting to tell us their story.

# 1

# Bread Crumbs: Things That Speak of Worth

BIGGER IS NOT better. It's just bigger.

The world would have us believe otherwise, as if worth is found only in great things. Bigger bank accounts are worth more than meager ones. Movies with more viewers are worth more financially. Books that sell more copies are worth more to publishers.

Even faith communities are not immune from biting on the bait of bigger is better. A casual survey of the number of books and seminars offered to clergy of all denominations on how to grow your church and all manner of ways to increase your stewardship speaks volumes about what even churches find worthy.

Worth, in fact, is most associated with monetary value or some kind of payoff. "Is it worth anything?" someone asks an appraiser on *Antiques Roadshow*, a television program on which people bring things found in attics and closets or stuck on shelves, relics from a trip, or an inheritance, or one of those "I'm not even sure where this came from" stories. The appraiser then tells the people what they have and assigns a value. Some things end up being of astronomical monetary value; others are worth a few dollars.

When you look around your home, what things do you think have worth? Perhaps it's an antique piece of furniture that you splurged on, but it sure looks amazing in your living room. Financial worth is one measure of value. Then again, when we think about what is *most* valuable to us, we recognize that worth is almost never about money. When we survey our lives for worth, we may note the things that are monetarily valuable, yes. But I suspect most of us see more worth in the people, the stories, and the values we hold dear. Sometimes we are fortunate enough to have some *thing*—some tangible reminder—of the person, the story, the belief that is of such great value to us. When that happens, the value of that thing is incalculable.

What small things of worth—this worth that is beyond a financial windfall—do you have? Maybe it's a photo of you and a friend that, if it catches your gaze on even your worst days, still makes you smile. Maybe it's your child's, grandchild's, or nephew's artwork, a somewhat Picassoesque drawing of you on the refrigerator. Maybe it's a shell picked up on the beach where the salt water and salt air honored your tears one night as you wept for the first time after a loved one died.

The big things in my own life are often represented by small, seemingly trivial items. Smallness, then, seems to have great presence. Small things can represent the great memories and the big moments.

I wonder whether we underestimate the value of smallness when it comes to how we experience God. Do we think of God only as large and imposing? Do we hold ourselves to excessive standards of prominence and high value when it comes to the life of faith? Or do we see worth in the crumbs?

For all the holy things we humans find worth in, crumbs are likely not high on the list.

They are what's left of bread, mainly—miniscule pieces from when we've sliced bread or broken it to share. We may even see crumbs as annoying bits that fall into crevices and that we need to sweep up. A good crusty bread, when we break off a piece, naturally produces what seems like millions of crumbs. We eat the bread, savoring it, but then we dust off the crumbs. Those small things fall away to the ground, unneeded and discarded.

Yet a resourceful cook knows the value of crumbs. Swept together, ground down from small pieces gone stale, crumbs offer a way to add depth to another food. Through the centuries, cooks have used crumbs to coat foods, to add flavor, and to stretch smaller amounts of meat into a more substantial meal. Bread that has gone slightly stale makes delicious crumbs that can be collected and repurposed and added to improve and expand the food that nourishes us.

Tamar Adler, chef and essayist, writes of the many ways to see small, unused pieces of food, the leftover crumbs, as a source of value for tasty meals. "The bones and shells and peels of things are where a lot of their goodness resides," writes Adler in *An Everlasting Meal: Cooking with Economy and Grace*. "The skins of onions, green tops from leeks, stems from herbs must all be swept directly into a pot instead of the garbage. Along with the bones from a chicken, raw or cooked, they are what it takes to make chicken stock, which you need never buy, once you decide to keep its ingredients instead of throwing them away. If you have bones from fish, it's fish stock. If there are bones from pork or lamb, you will have pork or lamb stock."

Adler didn't invent the value of crumbs and pieces and parts that are too often discarded as without worth, but she reminds us of it. Crumbs have great value, at least when we're willing to recognize their worth.

Holy creativity reminds us that a bit of imagination and insight can render a small thing into a great feast. God, like a good cook, has a pattern of recognizing the worth of those things that are minuscule, seemingly unimportant, and that we too often dismiss or cast aside. God loves to see the small things we overlook or discard as immensely holy. Throughout Scripture, God finds worth in those people whom the culture discards or ignores: women, second sons, and shepherds among them.

Perhaps we see the smallness of our home, our paycheck, or our ambition and question their worth—or even *our* worth. But if we pay attention to the crumbs of faith and of life, we may find God speaking to us in the small things, reminding us of the worth of things we might be quick to discard.

Episcopal churches use *The Book of Common Prayer*, a collection of prayers and liturgies, as the foundation of worship. Tucked within it is the Prayer of Humble Access, which says:

> *We do not presume to come to this thy Table, O merciful Lord, trusting in our own righteousness, but in thy manifold and great mercies. We are not worthy*

> *so much as to gather up the crumbs under thy Table. But thou art the same Lord, whose property is always to have mercy. Grant us therefore, gracious Lord, so to eat the flesh of thy dear Son Jesus Christ, and to drink his blood, that we may evermore dwell in him, and he in us. Amen.*

This prayer isn't a popular one in most churches. I suspect the idea that we are not worthy to gather up the crumbs under God's table is to blame for that. Not being worthy to sit at God's table is harsh enough, but not even being worthy to sweep up the leftovers? That, quite honestly, is a bridge too far. Surely, we think, we are not crumbs! After all, we are beloved and cherished by God!

Yes, we are beloved and cherished. But that does not preclude us from also acknowledging our inherent smallness, our inherent crumbiness.

For crumbs we are. When taken on a universal scale, humans are miniscule, although we love to pretend we take up much more space than we do. All that we have ever done and will ever do is a crumb when we consider the eons that have passed from the moment God spoke creation into existence with the big bang of God's voice. So, yes, even the most powerful human is, in the great scheme of things, a crumb within all creation.

We can experience this truth in different ways. We can wallow in feelings of insignificance that move us toward a sense of nihilism. Or we can let this humility dwell in our souls and enrich us. Like the crumbs that enrich meats and vegetables into something more than they are on their own, our smallness can nourish us as well. Remembering that we are but crumbs can lend us a perspective that deepens and frees us.

Crumbs have a long, holy history. That prayer in *The Book of Common Prayer*, the Prayer of Humble Access, was likely composed by Thomas Cranmer in the sixteenth century as part of the first prayers in English for people in England to pray in communal worship. Plus it has its roots in the first century, in people's encounters with Jesus in the Gospels of Matthew and Mark.

In Matthew, a centurion comes to plead with Jesus to heal his servant. He acknowledges his unworthiness to God Incarnate. He says to Jesus, "Lord, I am not worthy to have you come under my roof" (Matthew 8:8) and then goes on to share just how important he is in the Roman world.

Yet the centurion does not believe his own hype. He does not find his worth in his powerful identity as a soldier in the mighty Roman army. Instead, he recognizes that he is not all that. Confessing how unworthy he is in the presence of Jesus, he embraces his crumbiness, his humility, even his smallness in the face of great need. Perhaps this insight has come just in this moment, when a beloved servant is dying. Or perhaps this is a humility he has embodied each day of his life. The account in Matthew isn't all that clear. What *is* clear is that Jesus heals the centurion's servant and commends the soldier's faith and insight into his own crumbiness.

The Gospel of Mark, then, anoints crumbs as a holy relic of faith in a different way. In this account, a Syrophoenician woman approaches Jesus and his disciples, pleading that Jesus heal her daughter. She is a heckler, a troublemaker, an irritant dropped into the crevice of an otherwise peaceful time with Jesus and his friends. Jesus's friends implore him (probably loudly and rudely) to tell her to go away because she's being too much. Those who have been deemed crumbs in our world are always labeled *too much* when they say anything that reminds us that they too are beloved children of God and deserving of dignity.

Jesus, who is a fan of crumbs and irritants, doesn't send her away. He does get into a bit of a heated discussion with her about whether Jesus's ministry extends to the Gentiles (non-Jews). Jesus tells her, essentially, that it's not fair to take the children's food and throw it to the dogs, thus implying that she and her daughter are little dogs (which was not comparing her to a cute little Yorkie but was indeed a slur).

She replies with persistence and even a holy knowledge. She *knows* that the world she inhabits considers her a crumb. She also knows the value of crumbs. "Yet even the dogs eat the crumbs that fall from their masters' table," she informs Jesus—and all who are sitting within earshot (Mark 7:28).

This unnamed woman, known to us only by her ethnicity and gender—both of which mark her as among those viewed as small and insignificant by many who inhabited ancient Israel—embraces the crumbs, treasures them even. She claims her status as a crumb and knows her own immense worth.

Because crumbs have value.

Jesus heals the woman's daughter, and we are left to ponder the story. It's an encounter that interpreters of Scripture often desperately try to massage. We so want Jesus to be the kind, benevolent good guy instead of someone who would call a woman a dog and resist an initial plea to heal someone. But in this story, Jesus, the bread of life, has a very human encounter, one in which he recognizes the value of the crumbs.

Even the crumbs are of value, the woman reminds Jesus—and us. And Jesus agrees. Whether his agreement comes from an insight he has long held or one that he realizes in that moment—again, Mark doesn't tell us.

The gospel tells us that crumbs have value. Even the smallest things are of great worth. And we would do well to recognize the message these small things hold.

The worth and value of crumbs is both practical and spiritual. Cooks have long known the wisdom of the Syrophoenician woman, and so has God. Smallness is holy. When we recognize the value of our smallness, we see the way that crumbs are given for nourishment. We learn how they are sufficient, enough, even necessary for filling, for healing, for dignity, and for love.

# 2

# Cast Iron: Things That Speak of Seasoning

MY SKILLET, CORN bread pan, and Dutch oven are all cast iron, and they all belonged to my maternal grandmother, Grandma Williams. My sister's set of cast iron comes from our Grandmother Brock. At least one generation before our grandmothers' used these pieces too. Along with quilts and family Bibles, cast iron belongs to the holy trinity of heirlooms in many Southern families.

Cast iron is a staple of cooking in the South. Fried chicken, fried green tomatoes, fried okra: fried anything, really, truly demands cast iron. It goes from stovetop to oven to table easily—just make sure you have a dishtowel to wrap around the handle to prevent burns. Many Southern chefs maintain that cast iron is really the only thing you should use to make corn bread or corn cake or corn anything. A bit of lard, some cornmeal, milk, a dash of sugar, and eggs: if it's not baked in cast iron, corn bread should get a different name entirely.

The value of cast iron lies in its seasoning. For cast-iron skillets and pots to be used for cooking, they must be seasoned. Seasoning cast iron means covering the surface of the skillet with vegetable oil—my grandmothers swore by Crisco—and baking it on low heat for a spell (which could mean anything from an hour to half the day). This seasoning process creates a nonstick surface with the carbonized oil. Cast iron has a rough surface with lots of microscopic ridges and spikey edges that create perfect dips and cavities for oil and fat molecules to shimmy into and settle comfortably for the long haul. Formally, this whole process is called polymerization.

That's the quick and easy way to season cast iron: cover it with oil and bake it. But a *truly* seasoned cast-iron skillet is one that has been well used, ideally over generations. It becomes the holy grail of pans. The more you use cast iron, the more oils and fats fill in the gaps, and the smoother and richer the surface becomes. Older, in cast-iron years, is better.

Years of cooking in cast iron infuses every pore of the iron with fat, and fat carries flavor. The buttermilk- and flour-coated dill pickles, deep-fried in lard, leave their tartness and saltiness behind in the crevices. The molecules of red-eye gravy—a blend of the fat left behind by the bacon and black coffee—leave their acidic tang in the iron valleys. The oil that cooked fried chicken flows over the ridges and settles, so that a bit of the fried chicken from Sunday suppers remains. A scrim of flavor from each of these carries over for weeks, months, and years.

Indeed, every meal leaves its molecular trace in the skillet, intensifying its flavor and adding to its weight. The Thanksgiving giblet gravy—whose smoothness was coaxed and nurtured with a whisk, flour, lard, pieces of the turkey too many people throw away nowadays, and my grandmother's endless patience—seasons cast iron. The eggs scrambled with a touch of the bacon renderings my grandmother kept in a Folgers red coffee tin on the back edge of her stove: these season cast iron.

On the day after my grandmother died, we gathered and my aunt made eggs for us. My grandmother never served a breakfast of simply eggs. Breakfasts in small-town Mississippi were substantial events because lunch was light and work was laborious. Those breakfasts always included some meat, usually bacon, which releases its rich fat while cooking. The fat embedded itself into the cast iron. So it was that the morning after my grandmother died, fresh eggs—scrambled in a pan that had been seasoned by years of my grandmother's cooking—fed us.

Somewhere in there we could taste the grief, seasoning it all.

Like cast iron, our lives are seasoned with moments that settle into the crevices of our souls. All the particles and fragments from our own lives and from the lives of our ancestors flavor our days. And I mean *all* the particles and fragments.

We live in a culture that is enamored with the good stuff: the things that taste of happiness and pleasure. Social media influencers admonish us to cultivate joy. We are pummeled with ways to increase our bliss, to live our best lives, and to manifest our best selves. Surely, then, we can't have any residue of the particles and fragments of seasonings that are bitter, sour, even rancid.

When we do taste the bitter, the unpleasant, our world tells us to scrub and soak ourselves until all those flavors are gone. Certainly we can't be our best selves with flavors that aren't palatable. When they don't go away after a good washing, we may try any number of ways to rid ourselves of the seasonings that don't taste good to our selves and our souls, to cover them with stronger flavors, tastes that are nice and pretty, decorated with flowers and frills.

We may even try to throw away the thing that holds all those seasonings: the photograph of a parent who was so broken they made a mess of love; the diary in which we wrote of our dreams that people laughed at (so we eventually laughed too and gave up those dreams); the ring from the marriage to the person we thought would give us our happy ever after but ended in disillusionment.

Sure, we can throw all those things away, and we can try to rid ourselves of those memories. But emotions and memories are like fat molecules in our souls. Memories settle and fill crevices and niches, and they are not easily dislodged. After all our soaking and scouring and scrubbing, all the seasonings of our lives remain, the sweet and savory ones, and the ones that are bitter if not a bit rancid.

Good cast iron does not let go of its wealth of seasonings and myriad flavors. Chefs and cooks appreciate the value of cast iron that has a multitude of seasoning layers on it. The multiplicity of seasonings that slide into our souls does the same for us.

God thinks that the wealth of seasoning is a good and holy thing. Like the permeable yet robust surface of cast iron, all of our life's seasonings settle in the crevices of the self to create a resilient soul. We embody all sorts of seasonings, both rich and elegant flavors and bitter and acrid tastes. All these seasonings matter to God.

The psalmist writes, "Taste and see that the Lord is good" (Psalm 34:8). There is a literalness in this, at least for those of us in traditions that value the bread and wine as holy food and drink given by God in the Eucharist. Taste was and remains a vital sense. Our spiritual ancestors also wisely used taste as a metaphor. What if tasting something could be a vital spiritual practice?

I'm not suggesting we go around simply tasting all manner of foods to experience God—although I did taste barbecue at a place in Kansas City that caused my soul to rejoice exceedingly. I am suggesting that we let the flavors of memories and experiences and choices—the choices made for us, our legacies, our joys, and our devastations—fill our souls. What would happen if we let them roll around our mouths long enough that we could pick up the bitter, the savory, the sour, the sweet, and the salty?

Life gives us so many flavors: joy, grief, sweetness, and bitterness. What seasonings enhance the present for you? What seasonings overpower still? What things, with their cracks and crevices, allow for the past to settle in, waiting to add flavor, to overpower, even to simply give some depth?

And what things in your life hold those flavors for you—those tastes that fill you with love or cause you to wince with grief? Are some flavors and seasonings too bitter to experience again?

Salty and sour are powerful tastes, too often overpowering the other flavors. Salt hijacks our taste receptors, making the bitter and sour overpowering to the point of revulsion.

If too much salt seasons our souls, our memories, and our lives, it simply overpowers all the other flavors. The trauma of life, the experiences that leave us broken and weary, the exhaustion of being human: all can overpower us.

God uses all the seasonings, but I suspect humans have a tendency to let the salt and bitter be the only flavors we taste at times. When that happens, where is the holy wisdom that can allow more flavors in? Where is the prayer I can pray to experience the sweet along with the bitter?

During a recent season of my life, I was tasting far more bitter than anything. The death of a narcissistic father had flavored so much. Too much. The saltiness of my memories of him was overpowering. I wanted to deny and argue with the world that I was fine. I wanted to eat something, anything, that would fill the crevices that were tainting all the flavors.

The Thanksgiving after his death, my sister and I made the short drive from Tuscaloosa to Fayette, Alabama, where my great-grandfather had built the Brock family home. As we drove on the back roads, memories of my father surfaced, and I felt bitter and sad as I thought about his choices. Being carsick would have been more pleasant. I reasoned that perhaps this final trip to the family homestead would allow me to truly taste all the bitter seasonings and to finally leave them there.

For the previous decade, the Brock family house had been mostly quiet, locked up when the family member who owned it could no longer make the regular trip from her Michigan home to visit. Finally, she'd agreed to sell it.

As happens with many family homes, deaths had resulted in an ever-growing collection of items. Over the generations, things had simply gotten packed and stored in the rooms until some elusive time in the future, when someone might want them.

Except we all forgot what was there, and no one wanted the things. So there the family home stood, holding memories of the past. Both items well used and items well ignored by ancestors remained there, waiting, until the appointed time.

That appointed time was now, before the home and its contents passed to new owners. My great-aunt had instructed my sister, Nikki, and me to come and see if there was anything we might want. Other members of the family would visit later. "But y'all take whatever you find that is of value," she said, after giving us directions on how to get the key. A neighbor had the key and would leave it in her mailbox before she went to work for her shift at Walmart.

Our mother wanted to come along. She longed to see the home of her in-laws, the home to which she had returned from the hospital with a three-day-old me. There we would live for our first few months together while my father was on active duty somewhere else.

My sister and I both wanted to see the space that we remembered as children. We wanted to recall summers sitting on the front porch, its concrete covered in a stylish layer of Astroturf. We'd swing on the porch swing and flip through the Sears catalogue while The Aunts, as everyone in the family called my grandfather's many sisters, gossiped and drank sweet tea.

Sure enough, the key was in the mailbox and the Astroturf was still on the porch. The swing was still there, newly painted at some point. We unlocked the door lock, and the deadbolt, and one more lock placed for good measure, and then walked inside for the first time in decades.

A glass figurine lay broken on the floor. "I wonder how that happened," I mused to my sister and mother. "Maybe a ghost?" A raccoon or snake had probably knocked it off a shelf, my sister replied—and was likely going to run or slither out of a closet at any moment. My mom told us both to quit being weird.

We walked through the front room, through the dining room, and into the kitchen. Homes that have been unoccupied feel like a vacuum, empty of the noise and action that had ricocheted off the walls, floors, and ceilings for so many years. Seasoning yearns to be appreciated, tasted, and not simply left alone.

My mother opened the door to the back porch. "This is where your Aunt Nellie showed me how to hang shirts so they wouldn't need as much ironing," she said.

The smallness of the kitchen surprised my sister and me. Today's kitchens are often built like grand cathedrals capable of hosting royal weddings. This kitchen felt more like a roadside chapel: in theory, large enough for a few people to sit and pray, but in reality, large enough to hold one person at a time. Yet this small kitchen had been enough to feed our large family over the years.

My sister opened the oven—surely, we thought, not the same one from our childhood. But given its harvest gold finish, we realized that it was.

And sure enough, there in that ancient oven, we found the cast iron. On oven racks layered with residue from thousands of meals cooked over the years was a collection of cast iron.

Nikki nudged my hand with a skillet. "This one is yours," she said quietly, with that certainty that comes from listening to the ancestors and doing their bidding.

I lifted the skillet and breathed in. Immediately fried chicken, okra, eggs, and a thousand other meals all breathed out of the skillet. All the seasonings of my paternal family—the bitter, the sour, the tangy, the sweet, and the flavors I still can't quite identify—exhaled.

Time, as it does when we taste or smell a memory, folded into itself. Suddenly the kitchen was not empty and abandoned. Suddenly the kitchen—a small, functional, often sweltering place in the Southern summer heat—became a holy place.

Suddenly I was a child again on a summer Sunday as my Aunt Nellie showed me how to make gravy. I thought this was a sure sign I was grown up, even though I still had to use a step stool to see her cook. She removed the meat from the skillet and scraped the interior to loosen the good stuff. "Don't wash it out. Just let it all come together, and don't rush it," she said, taking renderings from the meat, some flour, and some water as she stirred. After several minutes, I held the gravy boat from the good china as Aunt Nellie ladled the deep, rich gravy into it.

Kitchens, in my family, and in so many families, are the inner sanctum in which women preside over the creation of all things nourishing. There they create dishes from recipes, almost all from memory and family lore. The kitchen of the Brock house was the place where my great-grandmother—whose job was listed as "keeping house" on a census record—made biscuits and cooked chicken for Sunday dinner, then judiciously and creatively used every part for meals during the week. Feeding a family that often had ten people around the table in rural Alabama, on the income of a farmer and an itinerant preacher, took creativity, faith, and no small amount of luck.

As a child, I had watched The Aunts shuffle around each other in an odd sort of waltz in the close quarters of the family kitchen, with windows open and fans blowing because air-conditioning wasn't a thing when the house was built (or ever, as I recall). They sliced tomatoes, dipped them in cornmeal, and fried them in cast-iron skillets. Dish towels that had been repurposed from Martha White flour bags wrapped around the handles of these same skillets as they got moved from stovetop to countertop to serving tray to table.

The gifts of God—in biscuits and fried chicken and green bean casserole and fried green tomatoes—for the people of God.

Four skillets, two Dutch ovens, and a griddle later, my sister and I walked out of the house with our treasures. We also found several Corning Ware dishes. I was *not*, as I told my sister as we packed them in a box, letting strangers eat out of the dishes that fed our family for years.

As we put the key back in the mailbox and left the house, I realized how much I had needed to taste the seasonings of my father's family after his death. My father's choices and narcissism had filled me with resentment and, in this moment, I needed to taste the sweet as well. I needed the reminder that his family members had added flavors to my life and they all mattered. In a deep breath, the bitterness and saltiness slid into their places alongside other seasonings, but not overtaking them.

When we got back to my sister's home, my nieces and nephews checked out the cast iron. "Can't you buy this stuff new?" one of my nephews asked, turning over the skillet and wrinkling up his nose. "This looks like it came from the garbage."

My sister and I gasped as if he'd just taken one of the cast-iron pots and put it in the dishwasher.

For cast iron, older is better. Older is, in fact, *best*. Good cast iron is the old stuff: the skillets and pans and pots that have the weight of history baked into their pores.

Lest I or any of us think the seasonings of our ancestors' lives or even our own are so scandalous we can't mention them aloud, the collection of books gathered in the Bible reminds us that *all* the flavors that blend, mix, and mingle matter. The flavor is in the fat—the fullness of the stories, not the edited versions. The Bible tells stories of ancestors who were faithful amid all doubt and of ancestors who were blathering idiots. Men we call patriarchs were out-faithed by women who did sex work, like Rahab and Tamar. Mary Magdalene, too long misidentified as a sex worker, is the base seasoning for the entire truth of the gospel. The entirety of our story of faith is indeed a cast-iron skillet that has been seasoned by faithful witness and divine presence.

Seasoning bakes an ancient wisdom into our lives and souls. Seasoning reminds us that the fullness of life is not just the happy, joyful times, but the imprint of the stories that we'd rather not remember, much less share. Seasoning bears witness to the holy fact that we have all lived a myriad of stories, each of them adding depth. Trying to silence the fullness of the stories is like trying to pry the molecules of fat from deeply seasoned cast iron; we simply can't. We can try to ignore our stories, our experiences, and our memories, but doing so diminishes us and strips us of the richness of being human.

Taste and see the wonder of the past. Taste and see the way that all the flavors and seasonings of our lives are valuable, indispensable, and holy.

# 3

# Coins: Things That Speak of Scarcity

MY MOTHER'S FATHER, Grandpa Williams, ran a rolling grocery store. He drove a modified school bus to rural parts of southeastern Mississippi to deliver milk, flour, other necessities, and candy to people who were without easy transportation and nearby grocery stores. He frequently received silver dollars as payment, and each year until he sold his grocery store bus and retired, he would give my sister and me each a silver dollar for our birthdays.

We would put those coins in the safe places children find—in my case, a small musical jewelry box with a ballerina who twirled at a peculiar angle because I'd dropped it. Sometimes my sister and I would get out our small collection of silver dollars and marvel at them. They probably amounted to no more than about ten dollars, but to young girls, these gifts were astronomical wealth. We would dream of what they might purchase for us one day when we were grown.

On a few occasions, my father would join us in our coin viewing. He had his own coin memories from his childhood. My father and his brother had sifted through coins from the family laundromat with their father, finding interesting and rare coins and probably a few slugs here and there that patrons had dropped in the coin feeders of the washers and dryers.

Then my parents divorced, and my father took our little coin collection and his larger coin collection with him. He remarried, and at the time, I hoped he took our coin collections in order to keep part of our childhood—even part of *us*, his daughters—with him as he embarked on a new life. Perhaps they were tangible reminders of the moments he'd spent with us examining the various coins. Perhaps coins were a way he could remember treasured time spent with his own sibling and father and children.

My father had a substantial number of other coins as well. His six-figure salary over the years from his job at a bank, along with his legendary cheapskate status, meant that he hoarded quite the stash of coins.

When my father died, his wife happily let us know that he had left everything to her. Everything. Even the items that were exclusively his, or not even his, she kept.

"Not even a damn chair," my sister would repeat, shaking her head, until the refrain took on its own humor.

We were not shocked, really, that he had left us nothing. Whatever memories we had of coins from our childhood—time spent with our father looking at dates, listening to his stories about Alaskan gold coins, learning old terms for coins, like jitneys—had faded to almost nothing since he always chose watching football or working at his job over spending time with his daughters, grandchildren, or brother. He might have been the one person who, on his deathbed, really did wish he'd spent more time at the office.

I found myself wondering if, when my parents divorced, my father had taken those coin collections not as a way to remember us after all. I wondered if he had taken them simply out of greed.

Coins can simultaneously give us great material wealth and mask a life of deep personal impoverishment. We too often judge success by bank balances, the asset columns on our financial balance sheets, and our personal net worth. Our culture assigns diminished integrity to those who live paycheck to paycheck or who are unable to support themselves financially on minimum-wage jobs.

But, in fact, Jesus says the exact opposite. In the Gospel of Luke, Jesus, in his Sermon on the Plain, begins by saying, "Blessed are you who are poor, for yours is the kingdom of God." In case we miss the point, he adds a few verses later, "But woe to you who are rich, for you have received your consolation" (Luke 6:20, 24).

In other words, coins can simultaneously represent wealth and impoverishment. Jesus was acutely aware of how financial balance sheets are easy ways to measure success—and even easier ways to avoid paying attention to the ways we are impoverished. Our treasure can mask the ways we lack the treasures that truly matter.

I'm not talking about financial impoverishment, a reality for far too many people in this world. I'm talking about the impoverishment of our lives and souls: the places where there is a deficit, a scarcity of something that truly is precious. The truly valuable things—dignity, love, forgiveness, self-worth, and compassion—are not so easily measured. These gifts are valuable only when they are shared and not hoarded. Love can often be invested in ways that will never create a profit margin but will simply be shared and given away, sometimes to those who will never know from where it came. Sharing justice and dignity will often cost us personally as we stand with those who are cast aside. And forgiveness empties us of the wealth of bitterness and resentment, both things our wider society seems to value.

Buying the newest fashions and being told how snazzy we look? That's so much easier than years of therapy, which can help us admit that we feel naked and vulnerable and unsure we are worthy of love. Our affiliation with a winning college football program is a precious and fun association; it can also be a way to avoid admitting how much of a failure we feel. Those filtered and curated photos we post on social media, showing all the fabulous places we've gone? We post those to avoid looking at the images of us alone, sitting in an ash heap and wailing.

All these external things can be idols when we count them as markers of success. As if having hordes of coins means we ourselves are valuable. As if having a closet filled with the latest fashions means we are all put together at every level. As if being the fan of a national championship team means we too are winners. As if having others like us on social media means we are truly, deeply loved.

Coins can tell us we have saved for the future or that we can afford a vacation. They cannot tell us we are worthy. They are not a measure of our kindness, nor an indicator of how well we love. Yet coins may, in their wisdom, tell us about the parts of our souls that are lacking and impoverished. They may demonstrate the ways we fill up space that needs to be healed rather than filled with random objects and clutter.

Jesus, in his holy wisdom, invites us, over and over again, to pay attention to the places where we are wounded, broken open, and empty. These are the places in us that need help and healing. Jesus's ministry is replete with accounts of his healing those who are sick or suffering. People come to him for healing, and Jesus often begins the encounter by asking what they want and responding to them. Those who come to Jesus know they are in need of healing for a variety of reasons; a common factor is they admit their woundedness, their brokenness, their sickness. And they ask for help.

Too often, we don't like to admit we are in need of healing, and we certainly don't want to ask for help. This is why I suspect we all reach for less challenging options, like masking all those empty spaces, those places in need of healing in our souls, with stuff.

And the easiest stuff for many of us is coins. We can very easily, with coins, confuse quantity with abundance. They are a way to ignore the impoverishment and scarcity we all feel at times.

Coins have been a symbol of wealth for eons. About six hundred years before the birth of Jesus, coins appeared on the scene. Maybe they existed before then, but archaeologists simply haven't found any. Clearly coins were common enough that those listening to Jesus's stories and teachings, both during his lifetime and in the centuries afterward, would have understood their symbolism.

People in Jesus's parables search for lost coins and celebrate when they find them. In the Gospel of Luke, a woman has ten silver coins, loses one, and engages in some major housework to find the one she has lost. You can imagine her looking behind furniture and under rugs. She reaches to the back of the topmost shelves, running her fingers over dusty edges. She crawls on the floor, her face close to the dirt and detritus on the ground. She retraces her steps, and wonders, and probably swears. Perhaps she says a few prayers as she looks for that one, deeply valuable coin.

The writer of the Gospel of Luke says, "And when she has found it, she calls together her friends and neighbors, saying, 'Rejoice with me, for I have found the coin that I had lost'" (Luke 15:9). Clearly a found coin—and perhaps a clean house!—is a reason to have a party.

But think about that. The woman in the parable upends her house for one coin and, upon finding it, spends some amount of wealth to throw a party, feed her friends, celebrate with them, and share her saga: all for *just one coin*. I wonder if Jesus is talking not about the coin but the search for the untold wealth of love, often found in celebrating with those we love and in recognizing the value of relationships. I would scour my house into deep corners to search for those things. Jesus seems to agree.

Jesus also tells of people burying coins, hiding them away, and then getting called out for doing so. In what is commonly called the Parable of the Talents in the Gospel of Matthew, a man entrusts his coins to three workers. Two invest the coins; one buries the coin. Upon his return, the man points out that the least the one could do was put it in a bank instead of burying it and, in a way, hoarding it.

I've always wondered if what really got buried in that story was fear. The one who buried the coin said, "I knew that you were a harsh man, reaping where you did not sow and gathering where you did not scatter, so I was afraid" (Matthew 25:24–25). Do we all sometimes bury our coins because we are scared, frightened of investing ourselves in relationships and in faith?

When we invest our love, there are certainly times our investment will not be valued. We will offer something another simply can't receive, and the pain of rejection is very real. The temptation to take our coins—our love, our trust—and bury them is very real.

Jesus calls us not to bury our true wealth but to remember that risk is part of love. Hoarding our love is not love; it is simply tragic.

We could take all the times Jesus speaks of coins as simply being about coins: about how financial wealth and financial poverty guide us all in certain ways, mostly unhelpful ones. But lest we get too negative about coins, Jesus uses coins to teach lessons in love, especially about what we love and how we love.

And (spoiler alert) what we love is not the coins themselves.

Jesus uses coins to represent what we value. Jesus uses coins to describe things that we value above all: things that we cherish and adore so much that we save them and treasure them. We search for them and guard them, sometimes too much. But this very adoration of coins may also represent something we lack. In other words, we can value one thing because we are lacking something more important. We might value one thing we have exactly as much as we long for another thing we don't have.

Self-examination is holy but exhausting work. But it's worth it to ask ourselves: How might the thing we *value* guide us to recognize the thing we're *lacking*?

Jesus uses coins to ask us questions, sometimes directly, sometimes circuitously. What are we willing to search for to the point of exhaustion? What are we willing to seek so that when we find it, we can celebrate with those we love? What are we willing to bury so that only we can know where it is and protect it? What do we need to dig up as we remember to invest instead of fear?

In all these questions, Jesus asks the big one: What do we value above all else?

Oh, but we so *want* to say we value all the good things. We want our lives to be filled with credits of love, built through honesty, sacrifice, compassion, and vulnerability. Those things, though, are so hard to hold as evidence of abundance. They can't be listed on balance sheets or résumés. They are only felt, only accumulated, through stories and experiences and quiet moments.

Jesus knows that, which is likely part of the conversation he has with some religious leaders of his day about paying taxes. While there are political implications to this account, told in the Gospel of Mark, I also think Jesus is asking us to see coins for their very real-world implications, representing money that can and also cannot be useful for us.

The leaders ask Jesus if it's lawful to pay taxes. Jesus holds up a coin and asks, "Whose face is on this coin?" In one of his many moments of eloquent side-eye—in this case to those of us hoping that hoarding wealth might just be a holy virtue—Jesus asks us what we think that coin represents. "Give to Caesar the things that are Caesar's and to God the things that are God's," Jesus says (Mark 12:17).

So to Caesar, to the powers and principalities, to the retirement accounts and the utility bills, we give the coins.

But to God? God isn't interested in our bank balances or our net worth or this great stock we invested in. God wants us to give to God the things of real worth. Love, especially to those who need it the most. Kindness, especially to those who quite honestly test us the most. Vulnerability to recognize the places in us that are lacking, where love toward ourselves is scarce and the temptation to treasure anything and everything but our wounds is great.

Jesus's teachings around coins remind us to be careful about what we treasure. Coins, after all, are just metal; they're representative of a value that, in the end, can't be taken with us. I sometimes wonder whether someone edited out Jesus saying, "They who die with the most coins … still die."

Somewhere in his life, my father received—and embraced—the message that there was not enough. Not enough affirmation. Not enough money. Not enough love. Life often whispers this, repeats it, and even yells it to us. These repeated messages of not-enough impoverish us, and soon we find ourselves convinced of the scarcity of all things, from coins to love.

Our culture prescribes all sorts of remedies for impoverished souls. When we feel not enough, temptation invites us to reach for something, anything, to fill the space. The easy way is to reach for things and stockpile them, like a dragon guarding its gold. We grab coins, accolades, relationships, all manner of things to fill the caverns of emptiness.

The easy way has a great cost. We continually hoard and gather and feed our impoverishment with deposits of things—things that can never truly pay the debt of our soul in full. Grabbing and hoarding all the things becomes a solution to our pain, a diversion from deep soul issues.

After my father died, his brother asked my father's widow for the coin collection from their childhood. My sister and I asked her for our coins. But his wife ignored our emails, texts, and phone calls. All the coins were hers now. He'd left nothing to anyone else.

Nothing material, that is. In many ways, my father left us *plenty* of stuff to sort through—stuff that had no material classification, no actual substance. He'd had several affairs, and he had eventually married one of those women, now his widow. She'd had a son from one of her previous marriages. My father had found my sister and me acceptable, but only until he finally had a boy with whom to play football. My father saw his stepson's athletic potential, and so he spent his time and energy on this new investment.

Having a stepson who played football accrued a certain kind of wealth for my father.

I wonder what our relationship with my father would have been if he had stopped trying to hoard things—money, security, a stepson's imagined athletic career—and instead had been able to simply recognize the open space, the feeling of lack. What if he had given to God whatever scarcity and pain he lived with? What if he had spent energy searching for the part of his soul that had gotten lost?

What if we could all speak the truth about the parts of us that are lacking and wanting and left drained and empty by all the messages of scarcity from the world? What if we could hold a coin and ask ourselves what we have collected and stockpiled, as well as what we do not have?

Hard conversations about feeling not enough are costly, but not as costly as avoidance. Looking inward to the spaces that are wounded and finding holy ways to heal is costly, but not as costly as blaming everyone else for your wounds. Jesus's message is that coins will never fill our impoverished places. Only love can do that.

The holy response—and truthfully, the harder one—is to let the empty space speak. Rather than hoarding the coins, driving the flashiest car, or having the most impressive résumé, what if we could admit our struggle with impoverishment, both literal and spiritual?

As for the literal, our keeping too many resources denies others the practical necessities like food, shelter, and a clean environment. But as for spiritual impoverishment? Perhaps we can sit in the empty space and listen to the wisdom that God speaks to us there. Instead of trying to fill it with all manner of things, perhaps we can render this empty space to God. Perhaps it gives space for the words of love we need to hear, ingest, and truly believe.

An ideology of impoverishment tells our souls we can never have enough because there are finite amounts of the most valuable resources. It assures us that if we keep getting, collecting, and acquiring, contentment is just around the corner. Depending on what we consider valuable resources, this tenet of impoverishment may or may not be true. Coins, oil, gold, and other things are indeed limited, which adds to their value. Yet the valuable resources of love, of memories, of joy? All those are limitless.

While we can all be tempted to *think* we know this truth and live it daily, we are all impoverished. Impoverishment is a human reality on every level. When we sit with our spiritual impoverishment, we confront deep lessons about things: about thinking we don't have enough, about what things we value, and about what consequences result from our hoarding.

We can ask ourselves as we look at all the stuff we've collected: Are we trying to fill a gap, heal a wound? What if we were to notice and name the empty space in our soul and let God fill it? God is rather good at finding things of value to heal our souls.

My father's legacy was a collection of all the material things that filled the spaces he and his wife didn't want to inhabit. Whether out of fear or habit or conviction, they steered clear of any admission of lack—and in so doing, steered directly into a lack of so much more. The collections of coins—both the ones he took from us and the ones he gathered in the bank—created a clear balance sheet of success he could show to the world.

The coins that were the *most* valuable, however, didn't rate on a balance sheet. The coins of our childhood and of my father's boyhood were a reminder of who he was and could have been as an adult. We, his daughters and his brother, wanted to remember, with these coins, the aspects of a man who, while living too much of his life deeply impoverished, was still a father and a brother. While we don't have a wealth of such moments, we do have scant memories of his life that are funny and awkward and endearing.

And in my more grace-filled moments, I understand why his wife is unable to share. Impoverishment almost always means we see all things as limited resources, as if love were crude oil. In her refusal to give any part of my father's legacy to his surviving brother or his daughters, she can believe she got all his love. We, as his daughters, his brother, and his grandchildren, got nothing tangible from his life. He couldn't part with anything, even in death. Nor could his wife after his death. Not even a chair.

My sister, my uncle, his grandchildren, and I grieve the coin collections, but not really. What we grieve is not having had a father or brother or grandfather who valued the things of true worth. We grieve that his choices were always about filling the space in his soul with coins or football or affairs. We grieve that we didn't have more time sitting at tables with each other, as we did years ago, and sorting through heavy yellow coins and silver dollars and other things that spoke of memory.

"Look at this one," he'd tell my sister and me as we sifted through a pile of small round coins. "This is an Alaskan gold dollar. Your great-uncle brought this back when he was working there. He had a coworker killed by a polar bear. And he saw whales!" We would hold the heavy yellow coin and marvel at the shine. We'd imagine a great-uncle we hadn't known perhaps mining its ore from the depths of the earth or winning it in a poker game. In my childish mind, it was worth millions of dollars.

Or we would show him a silver dollar that our grandfather had buried in the sand at Gulf Shores during one of many family vacations, and we'd remember the day together. My grandfather would hide coins and let my sister and me discover them on one of the annual family treasure hunts. I remember running until I was out of breath back to my father to show him, excited to add another coin to our treasury.

Sometimes I imagine my father and my uncle sitting at the dinner table with their papa and a cache of dimes and nickels and quarters emptied from the family laundromat in Berry, Alabama. They wrapped the coins in coin sleeves to deposit at the bank, noting unusual ones. "Now, when this coin was minted, I was in a minesweeper off the waters of Japan," my grandfather may have said in his deep baritone rumble. I imagine two young boys listening, touching a world full of the scars and heroism of a world war as they touched through the date on a coin.

*Those* are the things of value: the memories, the stories, the moments, the glimpses of the person my father was before so much anger and shame buried him. We have those. While a coin can certainly hold memories, we can also hold the memory even if we cannot hold the thing. In God's holy way, we can hold the truly valuable memories of my father without touching the coins he valued over so much. We can carry forward the sense of the boy, the young man, and the young father he was, and the sense of who he could have been had he not chosen the way of avoidance, of accumulation. We can remember the wealth of stories of who he was when he was still able to hold on to the coins that were truly of value.

# 4

# Scars: Things That Speak of Healing

"NICE WORK LINE," the cowboy said, nodding in the direction of my boots.

I was at a book signing for my book about horses and spirituality at a book festival in Kentucky. I had worn my Western-esque dress, which looked like something Laura Ingalls Wilder might wear—if she drank barrel-strength bourbon and wrote books that got banned, that is. It was a perfect match with my cowboy boots, which was why I'd bought the dress in the first place.

I'd rubbed my boots down with some leather conditioner earlier in the week, but the scrapes and scuffs were still apparent. I looked at the cowboy noting my boots. His own were very well worn. "Work line?" I asked, wondering if I'd missed some classic Kentucky cowboy lingo.

He pointed. "Your boots. There's the line where your jeans cover your boots but the toes still get scuffed from the work: work line."

I stretched out my leg to examine my boots. Yep, he was right. There was a noticeable line where my long boot-cut Wranglers covered the shaft and heel, polishing the leather to a burnished light tan. Contrasting, the toe and vamp showed their age with scars of all sorts. Surface scratches from hours in chunky Western stirrups crisscrossed the mid-toe. Deeply etched cuts from sagebrush and dry branches that looked like dried blood wounded the leather across the outer edges of the toe and vamp. Guiding cattle through wide open spaces meant following them, often on the roads never traveled, but instead covered by all manner of natural spikey and thorny paths. Boots protect, and their protection leaves marks.

I don't make enough money to have a pair of dress cowboy boots and a pair of riding cowboy boots, so one pair serves all the purposes. Summers of riding in the Mountain West, working cattle, and generally doing all things horses meant I had unintentionally developed a work line.

"Work lines mean boots aren't just for show," he added.

Indeed. The phrase "all hat and no cattle" is an idiom that calls out people who are all talk and no action—people who dress for a part but don't actually live it. Some people are all cowboy hats and jeans and boots and have never wrangled a steer, moved a cow and calf to a new paddock, or ridden a horse.

At some level, we all dress for roles that involve some aspect of show and pretending. We all don personas for show instead of actual work. We wear business suits, ties, and polished heels to look professional, put together, and accomplished when we're scarcely holding on by a thread and are running on caffeine and a prayer. We spend huge amounts of money on outdoor gear designed for hiking, kayaking, and adventuring when we barely go for walks on the paved sidewalks of our own neighborhoods, much less the backcountry of Yellowstone. We dress for the life we'd like to live or the life people think we live instead of the one we're currently living.

Work lines on boots, though, come only from living. The leather is marked and wounded by tasks and errands and walking around. Life, when truly lived, causes work lines. Newness gives way to worn. Sparkling new surfaces are aged and scarred, in boots and with us.

Scars on our bodies are a type of work line. I've got some of these work lines of life across my skin. A scar on my index finger, a jagged small line directly across the pad, is the remnant of my three-year-old self sticking my finger in a soda can and slicing a neat gash across my fingertip. A scar on my face near my nose is a badge from a case of the chicken pox. Then there's the one across my right upper bicep that came from climbing through a barbed wire fence in Wyoming to get a calf who was lost and needed to find her herd. The calf found her mother. I found a scar.

There are the not-so-visible scars too—work lines on our souls. Living is work. Getting out of bed to begin the day after two hours of sleep because the baby has cried most of the night—again—is work. Creating boundaries to establish a safe relationship with an alcoholic family member is work. Forgiving someone who never vocalized any apology is work. Trauma gashes our souls open and creates deep wounds. Just as damaging, microtraumas can create thousands of smaller wounds. We humans also have a way of constantly lacerating others' wounds out of our own pain. Hurt people hurt people, as the adage goes. Generational trauma gives some of us scars for injuries inherited from our ancestors. The wounds are there, often growing as we grow, until we realize we are bleeding and aren't sure why.

All of us have scars, both lines across our skin and places in our souls where our protective barriers were cut or ripped or burned, revealing too much of our vulnerable interior. The body responds, growing fibrous tissue over the opening. Scarring is a natural part of the healing process. In fact, all healed wounds, except very minor scrapes, scar to some extent, even if we can't see the healing tissue with our naked eyes.

I'd never noticed the work line on my boots, and I'm thankful for the cowboy who brought it to my attention, noticing it as something worth lauding.

Has anyone ever noticed your work lines or your scars—something well worn about you or your soul that's the result of living, the result of surviving? Are you proud of your scars, or uncomfortable with them, or both?

What stories do your scars, both literal and figurative, tell?

Scars are reminders of our innate human nature to heal. Scars are stories written in our flesh. Our very cells regenerated, adapted, and knit together the open space on our skin to form a wound now healed. The skin cells that form a scar are not as flexible as the original ones. Perhaps it's our cellular wisdom reminding us of past encounters: *pay a bit more attention next time.*

While most of our wounds-to-scars are minor, many of us encounter wounds that leave significant vestiges on our flesh. Life involves catastrophe, and catastrophes always leave scars. Traumatic injuries, invasive surgeries, and significant treatments for some illnesses hurt us while they are healing us.

We live in a culture much more interested in hiding scars than extolling them. When scars from surgery or other treatments remain, the norm is to have some scar-mitigating treatments, to lessen or in some cases erase their appearance. Lately, though, many people are deciding to keep their scars visible. Women who have breasts removed due to cancer are opting not to have reconstructive surgery. "Going flat," as the decision not to have reconstructive surgery is called, is not only more common than popular opinion might suggest; it's becoming more acceptable. The scar across a breast cancer survivor's chest hearkens back to the legends of Amazon warriors who cut off their breasts to better use their bows. Fighting for our lives leaves scars, and women are embodying the ancestral sacredness of scars.

Chris, one of my friends who opted for a double mastectomy after her breast cancer diagnosis, remembers the discussion she had with her surgeon. The doctor kept imploring her to have reconstructive surgery. "But I can make you beautiful!" he told her.

"My scars *are* beautiful," she told me. She is considering getting a tattoo on her chest as well.

Chris's story—of a physician reluctant to allow the scars to remain—isn't unusual. One study revealed that many women aren't even given the option of going flat. It's as if minimizing our scars is the goal, along with erasing the memory of the events that cut us, wound us, and sear us.

But the beauty of scars is a holy reminder that we can and do heal. Our very bodies keep reminders of the healing—tangible souvenirs. Scars are the work lines of life, which come simply because we live and move and have our being in a world filled with sharp edges and slicing encounters.

We also have soul scars, those wounds inflicted by a world that too often perpetrates wounds simply to watch us bleed. These soul scars are far harder to see and far more serious. Encounters with the sharp edges of racism, sexism, prejudice, and bias of all kinds can result in deep wounds. These work lines of survival settle under layers of learned behavior, apologies, and responses that may seem helpful but really prevent healing.

We often ignore the wounds trying to heal. "No, I'm fine, really," we reply when we are very much not fine. Or we make excuses. "Oh, that's just the way they are," we say when once again a loved one has acted in a damaging and hurtful way. Or we laugh guardedly and brush away hate couched in a joke that mocks our gender, race, ethnicity, or sexuality. "It's just their sense of humor," we deflect.

These wounds—from the barbed wire of hate, of family dynamics entrenched in secrecy and excuses, of a society that tells us what we see is not real and that we're overreacting or too sensitive—are often left untreated, even unrealized.

Scars show that our bodies and souls heal. After all, that is our God-created journey: to heal. In the New Testament, we read in account after account that Jesus heals people. We notice that Jesus doesn't simply walk up and inflict his healing upon people uninvited. Instead, we notice a pattern in which people approach Jesus and show him their wounds, their impairments, and their injuries. Then they (or their caretakers) ask for healing. The model suggests that God wants us to be involved in the beauty of healing—which means we need to recognize our own wounds.

Unlike our physical scars, those scars on our souls can shift easily between open wounds, slightly healed, and completely healed in the course of a phone call or family holiday encounter. The work lines on our souls usually demand that we keep attending to them. We might give a quick glance to see that the gash from our father's complete inability to express emotions except when he drinks is nicely healed. But the one caused by toxic sexism? Yeah, that one's still oozing. Better find some ointment and a bandage before heading outside.

We don't pay attention to these wounds in our souls for a host of reasons. A blend of shame and embarrassment is a prime reason. Too many of us have believed the lie that having work lines from life is a sign of failure instead of a mark, truly, of accomplishment. We also don't particularly enjoy admitting we've been wounded. "Walk it off," we tell ourselves when we've been shattered by violence, sorrow, and heartbreak.

But these scars, these work lines of life, might also prove to be souvenirs of the holy. They're reminders that we've lived in our souls and skin and encountered some things that hurt us. Our scars are reminders that life is filled with things that wound us and that our bodies are created by God for healing.

Jesus has scars, and they don't magically disappear. All four gospels tell the story of how Jesus received these holy work lines. Jesus was crucified on a cross. Crucifixion involved nailing the condemned to a cross or beam until they died. The gospels also share that Jesus was flogged.

The resurrected Jesus has marks where he was wounded by human hands. In the Gospel of John, Jesus appears to all of the disciples except Thomas. When the other disciples tell Thomas they have seen the risen Lord, Thomas declares that unless he puts his fingers in the nail marks in Jesus's hands and sees the wound in Jesus's side, Thomas will not believe (John 20).

When Jesus appears to the disciples again, this time including Thomas, he offers his wounded hands to Thomas to touch. Thomas responds, "My Lord and my God."

Thomas recognizes the risen Jesus not because of his perfection but because of his wounds. I imagine the resurrected Christ with scars. I think Thomas was likely traumatized by watching his close friend and rabbi be tortured and die. He probably felt shame for how he had abandoned his friend. How could his friends expect him to suddenly celebrate the resurrection of Christ?

I don't fault Thomas for requiring proof of Jesus's wounding, which was also proof that his own pain and grief still mattered. Thomas wasn't interested in some magical, scar-removing miracle. Thomas saw his own scars validated in Jesus's scars. After all, if the Incarnate Lord has scars, our own scars are holy too.

Jesus shows his scars to his disciples and to us. He shows us the places where the trauma of the instruments of torture and death split apart his flesh, which has now healed in his resurrected self. Perhaps Jesus's scars run even deeper—those wounds from being betrayed and abandoned by his closest friends, those who said they would never leave him.

Jesus's resurrection reminds us that healing is a holy journey. The wounds of our life aren't a source of shame, but a badge of survival and love. Jesus has scars. We have scars. These scars are holy reminders of our story, and we survived.

Perhaps that's why I find the moments of listening to people gathered in the Alcoholics Anonymous meetings at my church so elegant. "I'm John and I'm an alcoholic." That sentence is a scar of its own. It's a moment in which someone shows us the place on their soul that has been deeply wounded and has healed or is in the process of healing.

My boots, even when I condition and polish them, will never look new. For a time I wished for a shiny pair to wear for book signings, for social events, and for when I wasn't on a horse or walking through sagebrush. But after the cowboy's insight on work lines, I've come to see scarred, skinned, and scraped boots as pretty perfect. They're evidence of work, of hardship, of life.

Scars prove we are not living a pretend life. We're not just for show. Our scars connect us to the resurrected Christ. We worked with God in the miracle that is healing. The wounds didn't finish us off. Instead, they are souvenirs of the truth that life is often hard and of the greater truth that God created us to heal and be healed.

To recognize the scars in our souls as marks of God's healing is an act of deep and vulnerable holiness. Noticing them takes courage, as does showing our wounds to God.

*This is my wound*, we say to God when we let ourselves become aware of our work lines. *This is my body, broken from life.*

So notice your boots, if you wear them, well worn and scarred. Trace the work line on your body and touch it, feeling your way along the story of how the scar got there and how it healed. Find an object in your home that is worn, scraped, and scarred. Treasure it, remembering the life you have lived with it, and reflect on why its blemishes actually make it more valuable.

Touch your work lines. See them. Celebrate them, these holy scars. They speak the good news of our holy capacity for healing.

Just like boots with a clear work line, our bodies and our souls are scraped and scarred. But we are beautiful, holy, and blessed. Our work lines affirm a life of love that isn't just for show. They are proof that we've lived it.

# 5

# Sidelines: Things That Speak of Liminality

FOR A CULTURE that loves sports, sidelines hold a deep spiritual wisdom.

Sidelines are more important to the playing field than you may first think. Players need time to rest between plays. Less experienced players hang out there to watch and learn. Coaches stand on the sidelines to observe and coach. Sidelines create a space between the observers and the playing field. Fans are in the stands, players are on the field, and people who are watching and working are on the sidelines. In many ways, sidelines create the field.

I'm an equestrian, and we don't have sidelines. But we do have rails, which serve to demarcate the show ring, where we riders show our horses, and the outside space, where trainers and team members stand and coach, support, and cheer. I may be the one in the arena on my show horse, Murphy. But wisdom is on the rail: in the presence and voices of my trainers and teammates reminding me to breathe, to loosen on the reins or take up on the reins, to let me know where the other competitors are in the ring, and to simply let me know I am not alone.

The rail is where I go stand after I've shown, to share the gift of support and to learn. For me, just watching from the rail makes me a better rider, especially when I watch my trainers show horses.

At horse shows, lots of riders show their horses and then leave, as if all there is to a competition is their own part. Other athletic competitions aren't so different: after your event is done, you and your supporters leave. It's as if when we aren't actively on the field or in the arena, we're done. But is the most important part of sport the doing, the contest, the competing?

We humans like the doing of life, the activity, the movement from one task to another, the feeling of accomplishment. When we gather with friends or family after a long absence, we often hear, "So tell me what you're doing," and we're expected to respond with a whole list of accomplishments.

Life, however, is also filled with seasons in which we haven't accomplished much, at least on the to-do list. Maybe we lost our job due to cutbacks and we tried to find another one, but we're overqualified or underqualified or the salary won't cover living expenses, so we're spending our days walking around the neighborhood. Maybe we are experiencing depression and getting out of bed, showering, crying, and therapy exhausts us so that doing anything else is truly unimaginable. Maybe we are simply in one of those seasons in which we are sitting on the sidelines.

Saying that aloud to someone who asks us how we are doing would probably be accompanied by feelings of shame or embarrassment. We are so acculturated to accomplishment that admitting we aren't checking off life goals can turn up the volume on the voices that tell us we are failing.

God, however, reminds us that being in liminal space is not failing at all. In fact, being in the transformative space of liminality is some of the most important work we do as humans.

Liminal space is both a physical and a spiritual idea. Its name, rooted in the Latin *limin*, which means "threshold" or "doorway," suggests physical in-betweenness. Spiritually, liminal space suggests that we've left where we were but we haven't reached our destination. Liminal space is holy.

Sidelines are liminal spaces. They allow for watching, learning, and a participation that is deeply holy. Sidelines remind us that we don't always need to be on the field or in the arena or in the throes of life. We instead need to rest, to watch, to learn, to support, or to coach. In fact, if we think we always need to be working, playing, showing, and doing, we lose the meaning and value of rest, of Sabbath. Time on the sidelines can be holy time: time to settle into the wisdom that indeed the world can exist without our participation.

What thing in your life reminds you to stop, to rest, to be passive for a while? What speaks not of doing but of being? What speaks of liminality?

What might a spirituality of the sidelines look like?

In the Christian tradition, the transfiguration is a powerful moment of sidelines. Jesus and three disciples, Peter, James, and John, venture up a mountain. During the transfiguration, the disciples see and hear all manner of fascinating, mind-blowing, and confusing things.

There Jesus's "face shone like the sun, and his clothes became bright as light" (Matthew 17:2). The great prophet Elijah and the great patriarch Moses both appear, presumably out of nowhere, and chat with Jesus. The voice of God adds to the event, saying, "This is my son, with whom I am well pleased."

Peter gets really excited about what he's seen and wants to build booths so that they can stay up there. Perhaps Peter is feeling sidelined by the drama taking place before him and he wants to *do* something. He doesn't want to just watch. Peter has yet to learn a spirituality of the sidelines. To Peter's proposal, Jesus says, "No."

The Mount of the Transfiguration, or at least where we think it is, is, quite honestly, not all that otherworldly. It was likely mostly a scrubby forest. The trees provide some shade. The ants provide some annoyance. Now there is an elegant church on the site, as well as random ruins from some two thousand years of Christians doing exactly what Jesus told Peter not to do. Don't build something here, Christ said. Don't try to make this fleeting, miraculous, mystifying thing permanent.

Liminal spaces aren't spaces of permanence, but we humans, the doing creatures we are, can't seem to help ourselves. The doing in liminal space, standing on the sidelines of life, is a different type of action. We'll see things that are weird and hear voices guiding us. We'll probably hear some voices offering unhelpful advice too. We'll also be able to see many people on the field, playing, while we're not.

All of these things make the sidelines of liminal space uncomfortable. Sidelines aren't places we should stay forever.

But they are a place we stay for a season, an afternoon, a time. Mary Oliver, in her poem "The Summer Day," writes about being in the moment. She knows, she writes, "how to be idle and blessed, how to stroll through the fields." She knows how to do nothing: simply to be idle, simply to be aware, simply to be *not* doing.

We all move into these seasons of not doing. We all have time on the sidelines. Are you in that season now? If so, what events have led you to your sidelines? Perhaps you're here on the sidelines because of an injury; you need to rest and to let yourself heal. Or perhaps you're here to coach, to support, to cheer on others.

How do sidelines appear in your life? What do you see from the sidelines that you didn't notice when you were out on the field? And how will you know when it's time to move out of the liminal space of the sidelines and back into the action?

The liminal space is a place of transition and learning, but it can also be a place where we can pretend and avoid. Liminal space is a place of transition and transformation but not a place of permanence.

It's not the best real estate upon which to build our lives. Sidelines are necessary, but so is the playing field, the arena, the doing of life. When our time comes and the voice of God speaks to us, "You're up!" we can excitedly run onto the field, ready to play, to get a bit muddy, to try. Or we can begin whistling and turning our heads away as if we absolutely did not hear God calling us.

Sometimes we stay on the sidelines, ignoring our yearnings, our passions, our loves, not because of other people but because we are deeply fearful of something. Maybe we're afraid of success. Maybe realizing the thing we've thought we wanted wasn't really the thing, but we've harbored the dream for so long that releasing it seems impossible. Maybe dreams, as they often do, shift and change with the movements and choices we've made. Maybe the reasons are so buried under all the stuff from our lives we've avoided that we can't begin to understand *why* we want something. So we just stand there on the sidelines, hands at our sides.

It's easy to get too comfortable on the sidelines. We can watch from a relatively safe place, converse with those who are on the field, and feel included. All things can work for good through God, as Romans tells us, and all things can also become a way of avoiding or delaying the work of faith and love and transformation. We can get a bit stuck in liminal space. The moment of knowing is just out there, requiring us to venture forth on the field or into the show ring and act, even when the action will likely prove difficult, even frightening. God uses liminal space to invite us to shift and change. Often these changes mean we have to release something to open ourselves to something new.

We humans are capable of avoiding the difficult work that comes with spiritual awareness. Spiritual change often comes when we realize how many of the times we've failed to love as God loves come from our own selfishness. We, in fact, do not want to confess the truth that we make choices that tangle and entangle. Love invites us to repair relationships, to admit our wrongdoings, and to try again.

We must all spend time in liminal space, between adventures and insight, between knowing and not knowing. Liminal space is an important part of our spirituality: a place where we can stand when we need time and wisdom to untangle ourselves or simply sit and complain while we wait until we sense the next moves. God loves liminal space because there we are often forced to wait and pray instead of developing an action plan. Sidelines can be uncomfortable as we wait for the moment God calls us onto the field or, in many cases, shoves us onto the field, letting us know now is the time for the real work of love.

We can, though, choose to avoid God's holy shove and stay on the sidelines, standing, watching, even pretending that this is the best vantage point. We can settle for the sidelines because of fear, because of our own stuff. We are afraid that we will fail, that we are not enough, that the damage we have done with our failings at love is so horrible we are worthless.

We can also simply be lazy. All of these things keep us at arm's length from the fullness of holy love.

Make no mistake: God is there with us, loving us on the sidelines. We can stay there all we want. Some people have been so pushed around by life that the sidelines are the only safe place they can be.

Yet we often don't trust that love is remarkably malleable and resilient. Confessing our mistakes, letting go of hopes and dreams based in smallness, and getting in the trenches of relationships form new ways to love. And to encounter these ways, we almost always have to step away from the comfort of the sidelines and simply get out there, in the thick of it all.

We need to hear God asking us to rest on the sidelines, to stay in liminal space. And when we are ready, we need to heed God's call to step onto the field, however cautiously. Both are acts of courageous faith. Both are holy places.

# 6

# Roads: Things That Speak of Usefulness

ROADS ARE A way to get from one place to another, which most of us want to do as quickly as possible. Other than complaining about potholes or traffic, we don't think too much about them. We almost don't notice them until they are closed for repair or jam-packed with too many vehicles, and then we're usually overwhelmed with annoyance.

Roads aren't things we deem deeply spiritual. Few of us stand on a road and experience a wash of the holy fall over us. They are utilitarian: used but not deeply experienced, and certainly not as a marker of faith. Sure, we see the occasional roadside memorial where loved ones have marked the space someone has died, and the occasional turn-off and scenic overlook. But the road itself? It's hard to see anything particularly holy about it.

Eons ago, Jesus walked on roads—the road most traveled, because in many cases, that was the only road. Roads less traveled were often dangerous and risky—hardly the romantic and dreamy pathways made famous by Robert Frost. Roads most traveled provided some level of safety and sureness. Jesus took roads for the same reason that we do: to get from one place to another.

In a world before GPS, the best routes from one point to another were often passed down through oral history, artful maps, and even songs. People often traveled in groups for safety, and perhaps even for the collective wisdom and company. Our modern capacity to travel on lone country roads by ourselves without much fear: this is a privilege our ancestors did not know.

The Gospels of Luke and John tell us that Jesus frequented Bethany, where his friends Martha, Mary, and Lazarus lived. In the time of Jesus, walking from Bethany to the Old City of Jerusalem took about forty minutes. Today, because of the separation wall erected by the nation of Israel to demarcate the border between Israel and the Palestinian West Bank, the journey is much longer. A direct route is almost impossible and impassable because of checkpoints and barriers.

A few years ago when I journeyed to Israel and the West Bank to pray in the places where women of the Bible lived and prayed, our small travel group went to Bethany. I stood, as tourists do, on the edge of this road, on the edge of Bethany. I'd stopped at the part where it connected to another road to take some photographs. It's an unimpressive road, barely paved, running between a wall and a rise in the land. Bethany is still a suburb of Jerusalem, much like it was some two thousand years ago when Jesus would walk from Bethany to Jerusalem.

Standing there, I almost forgot it was still a very real road until a car buzzed by. Several cars were parked in spaces that may or may not have been parking places along the edge. A dumpster stood empty with some random trash scattered around it. Power lines interrupted a pale blue sky, and a woman pushed a grocery cart filled with paper down a brick sidewalk. Cars, bicycles, mopeds, a donkey led by a young boy, and a few brave pedestrians used this road, which was well traveled but not well marked.

During several days of touring Israel and Palestine, I'd taken photographs of elaborate mosaics that were thousands of years old—stoic ruins that spoke, somehow, even though the buildings they'd been a part of had long ceased to exist. I'd taken photographs of feral cats and one fat rooster. Cats in the Holy Land will claim any place they want to rest, from an altar in the Church of the Nativity to a table where I sipped coffee. And the fat rooster, who lived in a monastery, surveyed the monks and their daily life from his perch. He'd crow at random times just to announce his presence or demand oblation from the humans he reviewed.

All these things I deemed photo-worthy because they were beautiful, different, even quirky. Most in our group took photographs of such things. We photographed these important, notable things that mattered to us so we could show them to friends when we returned or use the photos to remember all that was remarkable about the trip.

But this road, in all its plainness, looked like roads I've seen in the United States. Nothing spectacular or astounding: just gray tar dented with a few potholes. I was much more interested in photographing the several-thousand-year-old brick wall that ran beside it.

But as I took some photos of the wall around Bethany, one of our guides said, "That's the road Jesus walked."

*Yeah, right*, I thought. In the Holy Land, *everywhere* is somewhere Jesus walked—according to marketers and tour guides and people who want your money—or sat, or ate, or worshiped, or preached. Everywhere. Only the bathrooms escape the "Jesus was here!" pitch—which is a missed marketing opportunity, in my opinion.

The guide, I suspect, sensed my skepticism. He continued as I put my camera away. "In those days, *this* was the road from Bethany to Jerusalem. So this road is on the road bed that Jesus and his followers would have walked."

I still didn't immediately grasp this truth. There was no marker, no elaborately adorned cross with a slot for prayer requests and coins or golden footprints embedded in the road. It was just, well, a road.

A plain, utilitarian road.

I pulled my camera back out and took a picture of a road, one that was unremarkable and looked like most roads I've seen everywhere else. I still didn't think anything of it. Maybe the Holy Spirit guided my hand. Maybe I just wanted to make the tour guide happy. Whatever the reason, I took a few pictures of this very ordinary and plain road. We went on to the next site—which was surely filled with more impressive sights, ones worthy of photographs.

Many of the things we now drape with spiritual sentiments began as utilitarian objects. Candlelight can change the atmosphere of a room, creating a spiritual space. Dim the lights, quiet the room, and light a candle, and suddenly the room seems a bit smaller, a bit more intimate and holy. Candles at home or in church beckon us into a peaceful place where we can sit with God.

Yet we associate candles with worship because Christianity and most other religions predate electricity. To see inside dark Gothic churches or to pray the Shabbos prayers at home before eating, people needed light, and candles provided it. Candles were like our lamps: useful, light-producing, taken for granted. That candles also provide an atmosphere of holiness? That was just a bonus.

Letting our prayers be lifted up with incense is another ancient spiritual practice. Many churches for centuries have added incense to worship; it infuses the space and time with mystery. Scents trigger our brains' responses—of memory and worship and awe—and incense fills the sanctuary like the Holy Spirit fills all creation.

But as deeply spiritual as many worshippers find incense, I will forever argue that incense came to be a part of communal worship not because of any sacred aura it might lend to the service but because it was an air freshener, a smoky fragrance to mask the noxious odors of blood and sweat. In the Hebrew scriptures, the writers tell of burnt offerings: a religious practice across faith traditions in which animals, from doves and goats to large bulls, are placed on a fire either to be completely consumed by the fire or partially consumed with the remaining meat distributed to the temple priests and others. Frankly, the smell of burnt offerings—not to mention humans before deodorant was invented—likely was not a holy, ethereal odor. So incense makes, well, a lot of sense.

Form follows function, even in our faith. Holiness and utility are not opposites. In fact, even things that are utilitarian—that we use not because they connect us with God but because they help us meet our basic needs—can remind us that all things hold sacredness.

These plain things we encounter every day—roads, lamps, fragrance—speak of holiness too. We simply have to notice them.

Usefulness can deftly disguise holiness, so take a second look at the plain things you encounter. What do you forget to see? How are the things you use every day so useful that you have never approached them prayerfully? What of this usefulness might speak of faith, of sacredness, and of love?

Some weeks after that trip to the Middle East, I was officiating a wedding during one of Kentucky's many spring storms when the power went out. After waiting to see if it might come back on, the bride looked at me and said, "Well, I'm glad the church has candles."

We ended up lighting all of them. We lit the candles on the altar and pulled out the candelabras donated in memory of someone's great-aunt. We scrounged around and found tapers that had been used for previous occasions, and we handed them to the bridesmaids and the groomsmen and the congregation to light and hold during the service.

In the midst of pure candlelight, we gathered and prayed in a beauty that was both deeply spiritual and fabulously functional. Afterward, one of the guests commented that it might have been the most beautiful wedding she'd ever attended.

At home after the wedding, I paused a movie to freshen up my gin and tonic. The screen saver of my television came on while I was in the kitchen, and I walked back into my living room to see a picture of a road.

I took a sip and wondered if I'd inadvertently taken a photo somewhere on my trip. I must have forgotten to delete it, I thought, until suddenly I realized which road it was.

*That* road. It was the road from Bethany to Jerusalem, the one laid on the road bed that Jesus walked. It was nondescript, unremarkable. Just a road.

But somehow, with the memory of that candlelit church still fresh in my mind, I finally saw the road as the sacred thing that it is. I saw through its utilitarian usefulness to its holiness. In that moment, the road was made plain and profoundly holy.

Jesus did not walk on roads paved with gold, surrounded by people who were elegant and lovely who wore perfectly matching clothing with all the correct credentials. He walked on dirt roads alongside us, the roads we all used and still use. He was surrounded by people like me, who on their best day still make Jesus want to put his hand over my mouth to stop me from saying what I'm thinking. Jesus, the Son of God, used mundane, regular, and even boring things. And he showed us how spectacular, mystical, and extraordinary things like bread, wine, water, candlelight, and roads could be.

Jesus used ordinary things to tell us of extraordinary love.

Far too often, the church through the centuries has told us that for something to be holy, for something to be godly, it must be extraordinary, gilded in gold and silver and the blood of martyrs. It must be placed behind protective glass and brought out only on special occasions so that we ordinary people won't touch it and blemish it with our ordinariness. Shouldn't things of God be sparkly and holy and way out of my price range?

And sometimes things do take our breath away when we see them because they are simply so astonishing. The Portico of Glory at Santiago, Robert Campin's *Annunciation* Triptych, and Salvador Dali's *Christ of St. John of the Cross* are a few that come to my mind. You likely have your own list of things that produce awe: those pieces of art, those buildings, those sunsets.

Our faith, though, is not lived only in the moments of the extraordinary. Our faith is lived in the ordinary, the day-to-day, the regular, and the plain. Our faith is lived with our ordinary friends, in our ordinary routines, on ordinary roads.

I stood there, thinking about this random photo, looking at it, really looking at it. Does the fact that Jesus walked on this actual road (or the bed where the road now is) change the nature of that road for me? Underneath the tar and asphalt and sand and gravel—underneath the layers that humans have added through the centuries—is dirt packed by thousands of years of feet, wagon wheels, and hooves. On that dirt the very feet of Jesus walked.

In this moment, I understood that holiness is also usefulness. God frequently takes useful stuff—dirt, water, bread, candlelight, even roads—to remind us that the holiest things are never those that are gilded and bejeweled and encased away.

Nope. The holiest things are often the most useful things. They are the items we use day in and day out, almost without noticing. They are the lights, both electrical and flames, that light our rooms. They are the friends we've had for so long we almost forget how present they are. They are the roads we walk on, bike on, or drive on each day that get us to the places we need to go. With God, all things are extraordinary.

What thing do you see around you that you often take for granted? Maybe it's the light switch that allows you to turn a light on to read, or the bed that offers rest, or the window that lets you see the world. How do ordinary things become portals to the extraordinary? And how do these extraordinarily ordinary things speak to you about faith?

There is a road I can see from my front windows. In the early morning I watch people walk their dogs. I see an older boy who walks a younger girl—his sister, I guess—to school. Every morning, while I am still drinking my coffee, before the sun comes up, two older women jog by, no matter the weather: rain, shine, ice, or snow. One day I watched a possum stroll across it.

Because of that road in Bethany, I have a new appreciation for the holiness of *this* road. Roads are useful, and useful is holy. This road in front of my house is filled with holy movement.

Our spiritual lives are also filled with movement. In fact, I wonder if the lifeblood of faith is movement. We don't set up housekeeping in one particular spiritual place and stay there forever, enamored with our vantage point and insight. Roads remind me that faith is not a place of eternal comfort, but an almost constant journey between places. Some of the journeys we walk so frequently they become deeply familiar. We know the way innately. Others are new, and we take each step cautiously and tentatively, praying we run into a group traveling our same direction for the company and the security. Some of our roads wind and twist between deeply awe-inspiring views.

The road of Jesus is rarely paved, often winding, and filled with potholes that remind us to take our time. Faith is not an express lane. It is often slow and plodding.

And it has been that way ever since the beginning. Eve and Adam moved, as a consequence of their own hubris and ill-advised listening, from the Garden of Eden to a harsher world. Sarah and Abraham and Hagar and Abraham's entourage moved from the land of Ur to newness, on a journey rife with more than a few mistakes. Mary, upon discovering she would be the mother of God, immediately set out on a walk to the hill country to see her cousin, Elizabeth. A consistently holy response to God is movement.

I often want to imagine myself journeying in a brand-new way, exploring new lands. I want to fill my spiritual journey with the extraordinary and the amazing. Isn't that so much more exciting than the ordinary and useful?

Yet God loves the ordinary and useful. That photo of a road I almost didn't take a picture of because it was so plain: it reminds me of the epiphanies that await us when we change the way we see ordinary, useful things.

# 7

# Calendars: Things That Speak of Accounts

I STILL USE a paper calendar. The first moment I spend with a brand-new calendar is fleeting and euphoric. Clean, clear pages testify to possibility. The spaces around each day and date are voluminous. It's all bare opportunity.

Then, slowly, I mar this newness. I write my name and phone number in it, claiming this part of the space–time continuum as mine. I note appointments and standing obligations: the church vestry meeting on the third Tuesday of each month, my regular dental cleaning and dermatologist appointments, my Wednesday night riding at the barn. Then I note the variable and sometimes singular events: the vacation I planned to Paris because the airfare was ridiculously low, our special Advent and Christmas services.

For a moment, I note the vacancy that remains—this expanse of new time waiting to unfold. Those spaces will inevitably be filled as weeks and months go by. After all, that's what calendars are for: to keep track of time soon to be claimed.

I'm not tech adverse, and I'm not coming for your digital calendar. I just think there's something holy about touching the pages of a calendar. Sometimes I tape pieces of events from the year on certain dates. When reviewing the year, I flip open my calendar to find my ticket to the Louvre, the reminder I scribbled to myself to call a friend on the first anniversary of her divorce, the taped-in prayer card I picked up at a funeral with a Bible verse.

Most of us think of our new calendars, digital or paper, in the January-to-December time frame for a year. But that ordering of time is a relatively new concept. The earliest calendars were solar and lunar. Prehistoric humans developed methods of timekeeping. When writing developed somewhere about the Bronze Age, so did a recognizable concept of what is now our modern calendar. Early calendars involved deep awareness of the phases of the moon, the sun, and the agricultural year.

The Romans, with their world domination, brought us all the 365-day year and what eventually became the names of the months we use. Known as the Julian calendar, it worked okay—except for that pesky fact that the rotation of the earth around the sun isn't exactly 365.25 days. So as the years went on, several people noted that the calendar had shifted several days.

The church found this particularly problematic as Easter is celebrated on the Sunday closest to the spring equinox. Easter was moving earlier and earlier in March, yet Easter is the feast of new birth and resurrection. So the Gregorian calendar came into being in 1582. Now, some 350 years later, almost every country has adopted its use.

Local ways of keeping time still keep us, however. The Orthodox Church still uses the Julian calendar, which is why its Lent and Easter celebrations are often different from those of Western churches. Judaism has its own calendar, as do most other major religions, including Islam and Buddhism. Different cultures also keep different calendars; think of the Lunar New Year in China. What seems like a commonality—the January-through-December calendar year—is really just one of the many different ways humanity marks time.

The word *calendar* comes from a Latin word that means account book. Calendars help us account for our days, our meetings, our obligations. Our ancestors saw these obligations as deeply embedded in the cycles of the natural world. After all, they were using calendars to know when to plant their wheat and corn, when the seasons for breeding and birthing farm animals were coming, and when to prepare for the coming winter.

Their calendars also marked holy time. The movements of the sun and moon that guided the calendar reminded people when to celebrate the end of harvest season, when to sacrifice to atone for sins or appease the gods, and when to mark the beginning of a new cycle.

Ancient calendars often intertwined a functional event (harvesting wheat, for example) with a holy event (a feast of thanksgiving). There was a natural balance of accounting that followed the seasons, a balance that sowed and reaped, that rested and worked, that rejoiced and grieved.

Our modern calendars are often heavily laden with the functional and slight on the holy. Our obligations are like an account that is too often overdrawn. We obligate ourselves to meetings and appointments without much regard for noticing the shifts of seasons. We fill our days with to-do items and obligatory celebrations that drain the holiness from ancient days of solemnity and reflection.

We humans are made to account for our time. Our ancient ancestors marked time with agricultural dates. We mark time with doctor's appointments and Zoom meetings. Either way, the desire is deep in our mitochondrial DNA. Our ancestors' calendars were etched in stone or were massive communal structures. Our modern calendars take up far less space than Stonehenge does, but they take up far more space in our souls.

"Teach us to keep account of our days," writes the psalmist, "so we may develop inner wisdom" (Psalm 90:12 ISV). The idea of account-keeping being connected to inner wisdom may be surprising, but it's a generative one. Our days and weeks and months can run together, and we move thoughtlessly through tasks and to-do lists. God invites us to keep an *account* of our days, to note them and reflect on them. To spend time remembering, recalling, and recounting. To see our days lived as more than hours, but as holy accounts of our lives lived in faith in all its joy and messiness.

Practices like daily journaling and keeping a diary are two ways we have of accounting for our days, but there are many ways. What thing speaks to how you account for your days? How do you preserve the story of the ordinary and extraordinary, the mundane and the meaningful, of a life lived with God?

My own calendars begin in Advent, with the new year of the Christian church. Advent begins in late November or early

December. The days are approaching their shortest of the year. The prayers of Advent speak of darkness, with all its holy wisdom and edgy danger. Advent is the season of waiting for the birth of Christ.

In Kentucky, Advent means that winter is settling in. My world often feels like it's getting smaller because the chill and darkness of winter mean I'm indoors more of the time. My great-grandparents spent the winters around a potbellied stove for warmth. My great-grandmother would mend clothes that were worn but still had wear in them. My great-grandfather would plan for the spring planting. They would read. They probably spent a great deal of time simply sitting in the winter silence.

Sometimes I imagine my Advent to be the holy time like they had: sitting, mending what has been worn out by the past year, being warmed by the time of quiet and simply being. Except then I remember that in my world, in the modern world, Advent is the lead-in season to Christmas. I spend it planning. My liturgy of filling in the new calendar, which I begin in mid-November, quickly reminds me of how precious and how limited the spaces on my calendar are. The season of Advent, a season of waiting, of preparation, and of prayer, quickly becomes a season of early mornings and late nights, of preparing for parties and gift-giving and holiday events.

Some days during Advent I've looked at the accounting of my time and wondered, "Did God resurrect Jesus so I could spend ten hours in meetings?" In sheer exhaustion, I've wanted to throw my calendar off the nearest cliff.

As much as many of us would like to live calendar-free, it is simply not realistic for many people. I lost my calendar for two days before Christmas last year, and I did not experience freedom or peace. I stress-ate chocolate from my Advent calendar until I found it randomly tucked in the pile of holiday catalogues from every store on earth that I'd been too tired to toss into the recycling bin and instead stacked on my dining room table.

After the great relief of finding it, I immediately flipped to the current week to see if I'd missed any appointments. And I wondered how a spiral-bound collection of pages marked with months and days and hours had come to dictate so much of my life.

Jesus says in Matthew, "Where your treasure is, there is your heart" (6:21). We too often default to understanding that verse as being only about money and wealth. And yes, that interpretation is important. But what if there's another layer of meaning?

Most of the New Testament was written in Koine Greek, and the literal translation of this verse goes something like this: "Where for is the treasure of you, there will also be the heart of you." Weird Greek syntax aside, I don't think Jesus is merely talking about what's in our bank accounts or on our lists of assets. The "treasure of you"—of all of us—is also our time: the way we spend it with each other, with ourselves, and with God. The astute and even uncomfortable suggestion that Jesus makes in that teaching is to look at our calendars and see how we account for our time. How do we spend our months, weeks, days, and hours?

How many of your days are filled with errands and appointments and meetings precisely scheduled to fit the maximum number of events in the most efficient span of time? How many of your appointments are for holy time: holy pauses, such as a walk with God and noticing the world around you, a block of prayer and meditation time where you immerse yourself in the silence, or a meeting with a spiritual director or coffee with a spiritual companion, a service with a community of faith, or any number of ways you spend holy time with God? Or do you just hope to find holy time somewhere in bits and pieces?

When you look at your calendar, what emotions surface? When you look at your calendar, what does your time suggest that you treasure?

Calendars aren't just an accounting of our present time; they also show us how we have treasured our time past. We likely glimpse the holiness of calendars in retrospect.

In the midst of transferring dates and noting appointments from the past year to the new year, I flip through my calendar for the past year. I see the schedules of events, of funerals I've officiated for parishioners, of dinners with friends, of reminders I've scribbled to pick up milk, the day I met my new horse, or quotations I heard that I didn't want to forget. I see that, yes, I spent too much time running around to commitments I should have declined. But there I see too many precious treasured moments, some remarkable, others mundane. Right there, accounted for on my calendar, are encounters with the sacred.

Calendars help us keep an account of our lives by telling the story of our days. One of my friends, who is originally from England, refers to his calendar as a diary. He informed me over tea one January day that a *diary* has a place for noting appointments, thoughts, musings, and even the weather. "We Brits love to record the weather," he shared. A *calendar*, he clarified, is the thing we put on a wall, with the days and dates in a block format, just to know what day it is.

If our calendars were truly diaries, a day's block wouldn't be simply filled with appointments but with reflections, ideas, or even doodles.

What did you do today that was unexpected? What made you stop and wonder if love would indeed win? Did you see joy in the ordinary? What made you think the world had gone to hell? What treasures revealed themselves on this day? And what account of it might lead you to deep wisdom?

Life is busy, often too busy. Days and weeks and months and years go by. Just as we review our year-end financial accounts, love invites us to review our year-end time accounts: the moments we almost forgot.

We live our lives in seasons, in seasons of waiting and expectation, of anxiety and hope, and of joy and celebration. The ancient calendars of humanity, both in our division of seasons and months and weeks and our religious calendars, witness this truth.

We, in our busyness, often forget to account for the very human moments. We become invested in filling the space with industrious uses of time.

Calendars frequently become an accounting of debits and credits for our time. Have we invested it in ways the world would deem well? Have we worked hard enough? Are we earning our keep? We allow the accounting methods of the culture to glance over our shoulders at our calendars to see how many billable hours we've etched into our days and weeks.

God, however, flipping through our calendars, notes how we've used blocks of time and whispers words like *Sabbath* and *wonder* and *stillness*. Holy accounting of time isn't a debit-and-credit balance sheet. Instead, it is a story told through moments.

What happens when you sit with God and look at your diary, your accounting of the treasure of time that God has given you? What are the valuable moments of remembering celebrations: births, marriages, new jobs? What valuable moments mark our fragile humanity and need to be noted: when we felt our heart crack into too many pieces, when we felt the prick of grief even after all this time, when we looked at our life and wailed, "Why?" What are the valuable moments when the day was empty and you simply got to sit and be present?

Calendars are holy diaries accounting for our days, months, and lives through time. They invite us to prayer. Touch the pages, now filled with ink and pencil and maybe even some crayon. Remember the days, the appointments you forgot, and the times you wish you could forget. Let the writings, the entries, guide you into prayer for all the ways our lives meander through grief and joy, through mundane days and magnificent events and all the spaces in between.

For where the treasure of your moments is, there your heart, your love, your life is.

# 8

# Shoes: Things That Speak of Vulnerability

WE ALL ENTER creation barefooted: slick and wet, covered in fluid from the primordial womb that births us. As we grow, our feet develop and change, allowing many of us to balance, to stand, to walk, and to run. Our bare feet test the world around us with each step. They feel the searing heat of August sand on the beach and the intense cold of February snow.

Bare feet remind us that we are indeed vulnerable. The soles of our feet toughen up as we walk and run. Our tender skin thickens with calluses from the friction of the skin against dirt, grass, rocks, and the rest of the debris that gets between us and the earth. Calluses on human feet have, through the eons, provided protection for this vulnerable part of our body.

But just so much protection. The archaeological record suggests that about fifty thousand years ago, our ancestors began wrapping skins around their feet to safeguard them from the cold weather and brutal terrain. Walking built up calluses, but our ancestors realized that they needed more protection because the world is filled with sharp, hard, and even dangerous things.

My personal history with shoes is a storied one. The process of shopping for shoes has been harrowing for me, even traumatic. My childhood and teenage years happened long before the internet, with its ease of shopping for difficult sizes from your own home. Odd-sized shoes existed in sensible loafers and practical pumps designed for the woman over forty, but not for the child or teenager with a long, slim foot.

Nothing fit. My heel would slip. When the salesperson asked me how it fit and I told the truth—it didn't—they would try again with a different style. Except most shoes didn't come narrow enough for my slim feet, and after several pairs, the sales clerk would give an exasperated sigh. The whole upsetting experience of shopping for shoes became traumatic when my father came along. On the rare times he came shopping with the family, he would tell me that the next pair better fit … or else. And I knew that everyone's life would be better if I just settled.

Everyone's life except mine.

One summer afternoon when we were back-to-school shopping, the salesperson brought out a brown pair of lace-up loafers that had a lion on the sole. They slipped when I walked, but the glare from my father silenced me, so I just nodded that they were okay. I stayed quiet in the discomfort.

I wore them my entire third-grade year. They rubbed holes in the heels of dozens of pairs of socks that school year because of the constant slipping. On the last day of school, I threw them in the neighbor's trash can so I'd never have to wear them again.

I had to wear shoes that rarely fit. One pair after another after another rubbed blisters on my soul as well as my soles. Shoes became a thing that told me to settle, to conform, and to suffer. Being honest would just make others mad.

I grew up wearing functional shoes that sometimes fit but mostly did not. Sneakers with two pairs of thick socks were a regular option until the warmth of spring and summer let me wear sandals or run free in lavishly bare feet.

I would have forgone shoes completely as a child except for social mores and burweed, also known as stickers. Burweed grows in the fall and winter in the South with a delicate, feathery leaf that carpets the ground. In the spring, burweed grows stickers with an amazing capacity to find the most sensitive part of feet. The Legos of the plant world, apparently.

Still, I loved living in bare feet. Mud and dirt slid around my narrow heel and between my toes. Grass cushioned calloused balls and tender arches. Running around in bare feet meant my blisters from the school year could heal. The earth fit my feet. That holy fit—bare foot on summer soil—offered an earthy sense of protection I needed.

Shoes, these things created for protection, did the opposite for me. I was a little human in need of protection, in need of adults to understand when I said shoes didn't fit, and in need of being believed.

Instead, I was learning, shoe-shopping trip by shoe-shopping trip, that speaking my truth was not safe. I was learning that vulnerability was dangerous, that it was better to settle, to agree, to comply. I learned to protect myself. Protection, then, became as painful as vulnerability.

Lessons we learn about vulnerability and protection as children stay with us. They imprint on us, and they become very hard to relearn as we grow.

Tao Te Ching said, "When the student is ready, the teacher will appear." I'm not sure I was completely ready when a local drag queen who attended the New York church where I served introduced me to a shoe store. But I'm grateful they appeared.

The shoe shop specialized in different sizes and widths. "It's where lots of drag queens get their shoes," they told me, pointing down to the snazzy red pumps they'd worn for our Pentecost celebration.

So off I went to the store on Fifth Avenue, and soon I found a pair of black patent leather Mary Jane pumps. The sales clerk measured my foot, and I expected the usual "We don't have your width, but maybe we can add some pads."

Except no! The sales clerk brought out a slim pair and slipped them on my feet. I took a few steps and realized they fit gloriously and perfectly. No slipping. No added pads. No anything extra! I didn't even have to lie to the clerk or myself or try to convince myself that they fit, because they did. I stood there, looking in the mirror at my feet adorned in a pair of stylish, fancy, mostly impractical shoes. They looked gorgeous.

I wore those black patent Mary Jane pumps to every dressy occasion. I wore them at casual events. I probably even wore them with sweatpants. And then I returned to the store and bought another pair that fit. Then another.

One day I realized I could take the shoes I owned that didn't fit and give them away. Giving away those shoes that didn't fit was the next part of a lesson about vulnerability.

Between an excellent pair of stack-heeled Mary Janes and a drag queen, I slowly began to realize I did not have to live with discomfort as protection. I could wear shoes, and even wear a life, that fit.

We humans, when our vulnerabilities are exploited and discounted, will find ways to protect ourselves. We will nod and agree. We will build defenses and learn to cry when no one sees us. We will settle for something that feels safe, even when what we consider safety is mostly just staying in the same pair of shoes we've worn for years, whether they fit or not.

Vulnerability means we need protection, even if just to feel safe about being vulnerable. And we humans are a vulnerable bunch. I'm not sure we like that truth about ourselves: just how vulnerable we are, just how tender our bodies and our souls are. How susceptible we are to the pain of words of those who refuse to hear and see us.

When we feel the pain inflicted by our vulnerabilities, the holy response is to feel that pain and discomfort, to sit with it and let it inform us. But for many of us, so much of this pain was perpetrated when we were too vulnerable, too young, or too powerless to let the discomfort instruct us.

So we did what our ancestors have done for eons: we found ways to protect ourselves. We pulled on shoes that didn't really fit, but we made do. We put on emotional armor to defend ourselves from hateful words. We developed practices and responses to keep the peace so we wouldn't be on the receiving end of rage. We created so many defenses, personas, and identities because we needed protection.

Some of the ways we tried to protect ourselves were profoundly helpful. Some were not. When we were grasping for protection and unable to find it, we wrapped ourselves in whatever protections we could find. There's a reason children have teddy bears and blankets and snuggies to embrace when the dark feels scary.

When you retrace your steps to a place where the world was risky or even dangerous for you, what made you vulnerable? How did you find protection? What did you embrace when the world felt too scary?

Maybe the object was a helpful one that reminds you of safety, love, and security. Maybe the object was helpful at the time but doesn't fit anymore. Perhaps that thing you grabbed that seemed to comfort, to guard, to protect did exactly the opposite. Those things often remind us of a vulnerability that was scary, that cost us part of our souls.

Sometimes, even, the things we grasp to feel safe are the very things that lead us to profound vulnerability. Sometimes God calls us to put them down, and we haltingly say yes.

When Moses encounters God in the burning bush, Moses has been wandering around in the wilderness—hiding, I suspect, from the life he left in Egypt. He is vulnerable in many ways. He's a wanted man because he killed an Egyptian who was beating a Hebrew. He has fled life as a member of the royal household to marry into a shepherding tribe. I can imagine he has figured out by now that the life that he was born into did not protect him as he'd hoped.

Moses has clothed himself in the protective accoutrements of his life as a shepherd and husband, probably right down to his shoes. The shoes of his Egyptian court life are long gone. Moses, now wearing the shoes of a shepherd, sees an unusual and even spellbinding thing: a burning bush that doesn't burn up. Maybe he's mesmerized by it the way we are by campfires. Entranced by this holy phenomenon, he strolls over and encounters God.

God tells Moses to remove his shoes. Remove the trappings of the roles you've embraced, God says. You've had reasons to embrace those roles—some good and some sketchy—but now stand barefooted in this holy place.

Moses does. He takes off the protections of his life and stands vulnerable before God.

In the Gospel of John, Jesus gathers with his disciples on the night before he is crucified. They eat a meal, and then

Jesus begins to teach them. Love one another, as I have loved you, he says. Love like this is deeply and profoundly vulnerable and unspeakably beautiful. It is the love that we as humans need to function and, more so, to thrive.

Then Jesus washes his disciples' bare feet. I've always imagined Jesus himself to be barefooted too. I suspect that he becomes deeply vulnerable in this way—even with those he knows will abandon and betray him. This incarnate vulnerability in Jesus touches the dusty, dirty feet of the men who say they love him too—and then will leave him bleeding.

Like Moses, like Jesus, we too are called to go to holy places of vulnerability in our lives of faith. We unlace, unbuckle, kick off, and toss aside the inventions that we assume will protect us. We step out of convention and expectation. We kick off the things of beauty that complete our outfit—the external costume we put on to embellish the roles we inhabit day in and day out. We finally take off the shoes that don't fit and let the bones and tendons and flesh of our selves and souls connect with the earth.

We may deliberately seek out these holy encounters. But often we stumble into them, having walked down roads that seemed benign at first, even exciting. Then we realize the prayer we've prayed is answered. God really does mean for us to love our neighbor as ourselves, even the one supporting a different political agenda. God really does want us to care for the outcasts, even when doing so means we have to venture out of our own comfortable places. God really does mean to love when love means we have to be vulnerable to those with whom we are in relationship.

When we encounter God, a time may come when God asks us to take off our shoes—to step out of the things that protect us and into holy vulnerability. God will ask us to stand in bare feet. God will ask us to feel the ground underneath us, all of it. Feel the softness that gives under the pressures of our heels. Feel the rocks that poke and stab. Feel the comfortable and uncomfortable, the logical and the mysterious, the rich soil and the slimy mud.

Stand in the holiness of bare feet and feel all of creation. Connect to the earth that God creates—the dusty, dirty, holy ground that God called forth.

# 9

# Rocks: Things That Remember

OF ALL THE things in creation we encounter, rocks are the most nearly eternal.

Rocks hold a deep intelligence in their density, presence, and wisdom. Rocks have been sacred to humans for eons, and all religious faiths, in some way, see holiness in these complex bonds of sand and water and time. The Dome of the Rock in Jerusalem is built over the rock where Muhammad ascended into heaven and where Abraham is said to have prepared his son Isaac for sacrifice. The Black Stone of Mecca is a shattered black rock sacred to Muslims. Jewish believers leave rocks on graves as signs of enduring love and for a host of other reasons. In the Church of the Holy Sepulchre, Christianity hallows the slab of rock from the tomb from which Jesus was resurrected.

During his life on earth, Jesus recognized the importance of rocks. He renamed Peter, one of his disciples, "Rock" and then commissioned him to build the church. Large quarried stones built the great cathedrals and small chapels. Ancient desert mothers and fathers—people who left cities to move to the wilderness in order to devote themselves to a life of solitude and prayer—used pebbles to keep track of their prayers and to count the psalms as they recited them. These stones became forbearers, in a sense, of the beads in our modern rosaries.

Both the places of Christ's birth and death are marked by large rocks. In the Church of the Nativity in Bethlehem, the lowest level of the church leads to a grotto. There, in the marble floor, is a hole surrounded by an ornate fourteen-point silver star inlay. In the hole is a rock where the manger holding the Christ Child supposedly rested. In Jerusalem, the Church of the Holy Sepulchre contains all manner of stones and rocks associated with the death and resurrection of Jesus, including the rock of Golgotha where Jesus was crucified, the stone slab where the women anointed the body of Jesus after his death, and the stone where Jesus was resurrected.

All these holy rocks and stones are surrounded by candles and gilded metal and other extravagance. Pilgrims whisper prayers as they touch them. Tears anoint them. They are holy.

And they are rocks.

These profoundly common things have a deep spiritual legacy. First and foremost, rocks have staying power. The oldest rocks on earth are over 4 billion years old, not too much younger than the very planet we inhabit. Rocks *last*. This steadfastness is a physical witness to us in a world in which so much feels transient and fleeting. The rocks we touch on hikes were likely around, in some form, thousands of years ago. Touching the stones at sacred sites is a way we touch the Holy, the steadfast presence of God that is not fleeting but permanent.

For all their permanence, rocks are also permeable, although not in ways we can see. We almost must accept this contrary state of existence on faith. Rocks are "Solid stone … sand and water with a million years gone by," as singer-songwriter Beth Nielsen Chapman says. They have an internal structure of inorganic matter compressed by time.

The story of our whole earth is told in the stories of rocks. Within an outwardly simple rock are rich layers telling the stories of time and season through layers of sediment. The very center of the earth is laced with rock, and the very center of our faith is laced with rock too. We stand on it. We kneel to touch it. We build with it. We create markers out of it.

I was thinking about none of this as I picked a rock out of my horse's hoof one afternoon in Spain. The mare I rode, Mala Reina, and I had joined a group of pilgrims riding the Camino de Santiago, the Way of St. James. It's a pilgrimage from various points in Europe and the Middle East that converge in Santiago, Spain, where the Cathedral of St. James (Catedral de Santiago de Compostela) welcomes those who have walked or biked or ridden. The cathedral houses the relics of St. James and has for centuries served as a way people journey a literal path to experience God's holiness.

We had stopped for lunch in a clearing in a Galician forest that part of the Camino ran through. Wild blackberry bushes grew in a thick patch at the edge of the clearing where we tied up our horses. I realized the ones near the top were ripe and plentiful, and I could reach them easily sitting on my horse. I ate some blackberries from the saddle of my horse before I dismounted for lunch. Checking my horse's hooves, as it's good to do from time to time, I found a stone, possibly bothersome to my mount. I picked it out of her hoof and tucked it in my pocket somewhat mindlessly.

After I returned home some weeks later, I added it to a crystal bowl that sits on my dresser, along with other stones I've collected over the years. I have a flat stone from a convent where I went on retreat. The nuns painted words on polished stones and left them in the chapel for us to take. Mine was in French: *croyez.* Believe.

In the bowl is a rock from the beach of Tel Aviv. It has a small hole in it. I thought the hole was some odd natural occurrence, but one of my fellow pilgrims in Israel told me otherwise: "Those were weights used by fishermen thousands of years ago." The weird little stone with the hole was, in my imagination, changed into a rock that weighed down the nets the disciples used to fish when they saw Jesus strolling on the water. (Never mind that it was the Sea of Galilee where Jesus walked on water, not the Mediterranean Sea where I stood in the chilly water holding a pebble.)

Most days those stones nestle in their elegant crystal surroundings on my dresser. I usually only move the bowl when I'm dusting. But some days, I pick up a stone or two, hold its weight in my palm, and let it remind me of a place or a moment in the past: a time when I reached down to ask the earth to loan me part of itself to hold a memory.

Yes, these rocks are souvenirs of moments, of places, and of adventures. Our human liturgy of letting rocks and stones remind us of the past—become placeholders for our memories—is an ancient practice.

But what if rocks hold their own memories too? What if these rocks, made of silicates, carbonates, phosphates, oxides, sulfides, and sulfates, hold a kind of memory that has nothing to do with humans—a remembering of this earth as it has been? What if things in the natural world carry deep wisdom about what this holy creation of God once was and once again will be?

We humans invest energy in memory-keeping. From scrapbooks to diaries, we jot down notes so we don't forget. Do we consider, though, that all of creation, in some way, remembers? Trees, in their rings, tell of seasons of drought that stunted growth, of fire that charred outer bark, and of blissful summers when cells multiplied and wood strengthened. Streams, creeks, and rivers narrate a tome of movement through the land, carrying pieces of earth from one direction to another, depositing their memories into each other until they tell their story to the ocean.

Geologists are experts at translating the stories rocks tell us. Rocks break apart, push against each other, and fall in layers. In this way, rocks write their lines in the earth. When you drive through most parts of Kentucky, you move through canyons carved for a roadway, leaving ribboned strata from eons of stories of the land. Limestone whispers of the sea life that lived and died here—tiny fossil fragments that accumulated and accumulated and accumulated. Coal seams underline the layers, black and rich and complicated. Sandstone brings space and air with its porosity. On an eastward drive from Lexington to Harlan, I can see the memories of millions of years.

Yes, rocks remember.

At least three-quarters of the earth is covered with sedimentary rocks, so it's no surprise that rocks became an easy and convenient partner of humans, from tools to building materials. Perhaps their ubiquity has made them seem even more sacred to us.

Perhaps, though, their holiness isn't something we imbue them with. Perhaps their holiness is something inherent. Perhaps their sentience is different from ours, yet still as holy.

Some Indigenous cultures see rocks as alive. Patty Krawec, in her book *Becoming Kin,* asks holy questions: "Are the stones alive? Can rocks cry out?"

She goes on to speak of the Anishinaabe understanding of land and of stones:

> *In the Anishinaabe universe, even before the thoughts of Kiche Manidou—the Creator, or Great Mystery—there was what Louise Erdrich calls "a conversation between stones."*

> *When I was in grade 9, my science teacher asked the class if stones were alive. We were learning the seven criteria of life. After reviewing the list, we said that no, stones were not alive. He asked us if we were sure. And so we went over the criteria again and told him yes, we were sure. He said that it might be that stones did things more slowly than we could measure. Could it be that we lacked the ability to see these things in stones? Or could the criteria be wrong? Then he smiled. I don't think my teacher was suggesting that stones are alive; I think he wanted us to remember that science is the asking of questions and the constant adjustment of what we think we know. Later, in physics, we would learn about how some matter exists as both wave and particle, depending on how you look at it. Perspective matters. This possibility—of something like a stone being alive—has stayed with me.*

Something being alive or dead is not necessarily a clear dichotomy. Yes, there are medical and scientific criteria for being considered alive. And our language uses the word in ways that have little to do with brain activity or capacity for metabolism. We speak of things being alive that have vividness—a painting of bright, strong colors is alive. An idea may be alive with possibilities when it creates energy in those who hear it. Aliveness can also mean the thing has an effect on those who encounter it. Being alive, in a holy, mystical sense, is about encounter.

When we consider whether something is alive or not, perspective matters. Relationships matter. Connection matters.

Krawec continues, "Anishinaabemowin, as well as many other languages, is concerned with the action and relationship—whether things are animate or inanimate. … But even being inanimate does not preclude something from having spirit."

Perhaps this Indigenous wisdom invites us to expand our concept of aliveness into a concept of spirit. Spirit, especially in religious traditions, speaks of something with life and energy and relationship beyond defined biological factors. The Holy Spirit of the Christian New Testament is defined in the Nicene Creed, one of the key creedal statements of faith, as the Lord, the giver of life. In Greek, *pneûma* means breath, an animating power, and even soul. The Holy Spirit, like rocks, has sentience that doesn't neatly fit into our understanding of something being alive.

For the Anishinaabe of Turtle Island, the Indigenous people of Australia, and the Sámi, an Indigenous people in Northern Europe, there is a sacred sentience of rocks. Many

Indigenous cultures recognize the holiness of rocks not as simply gravel to be used but as holy siblings to be honored. To move them, to collect them, and to take them from their resting places disturbs their life.

The Bible combines these concepts of spirit and rock into a powerful image of creation.

In Deuteronomy, Moses (or whoever wrote the text) describes God as a rock who gives birth: "You ignored the rock who gave you birth" (32:18).

What an amazing God this is—a rock who gives birth. God, as sand and water with a million years gone by, birthed us humans.

Jesus counters the Pharisees, who tell him to quiet down his disciples, who are celebrating Jesus's triumphal entry into Jerusalem. He responds, "I tell you, if these were silent, the stones would shout out" (Luke 19:40).

Rocks birthing, rocks testifying, rocks remembering: our spiritual heritage suggests that rocks *act*. They *do*. No matter how you define life, I think you can say that rocks are memory-keepers. They hold the past in slow, ancient ways that our souls long to touch when we reach for them. Their memories seep and radiate with a slowness that is imperceptible to us. That is indeed why we can so easily not hear what they have to say.

Krawec asks, "What if the land is a being in its own right?" If we say yes, then rocks are the memory-keepers of the land—of all creation, really.

Rocks, then, are something of our ancestors that remember. They have spiritual wisdom, holy truth, and even prophetic witness to share.

Rocks are an image of God that we are called to listen to in our holy places, whether that be human-made shrines that encompass rocks or the shrines creation scatters across the landscape. Rocks are the image of God who birthed us. Rocks are given the responsibility of crying out for Jesus.

They cry out to us still, although many of us have forgotten how to listen. In the same way I wouldn't take a religious icon or cross adorning a church as a souvenir, I also know there are places from which I do not take the rocks. I can hold them. I can listen to them. I also can leave them for other pilgrims to encounter. On the rare occasions I take one, I like to think that the rock has more to say to me than what I can hear in the short time of our encounter. And I return the honor by listening to what the rock remembers.

Rocks tell stories of our life and faith. Rocks tell their own story too. If we are in relationship with all of creation, we need to listen to them. Perhaps this harmony of complexity, longevity, mystery, and commonness is why we are drawn to them, why we need them as a touchstone for our faith.

For billions of years, rocks have shouted, spoken, remembered, and whispered about God. How might we better listen to the wisdom they share with us, the memories they hold, and the truth they witness? How might we listen to the testimony of sand and water, of magma and pressure and time?

# 10

## Garden Shears: Things That Speak of Pruning

MY GARDENING STYLE could be described as benign neglect. My specialty is herbs. My great-uncle Leon, a botanist, used to say herbs are just weeds that we've found a use for.

So, yes, I grow weeds quite well.

Somewhere during my years of basil, thyme, chives, sage, and oregano gardens, I've learned the value of a good pruning. Pruning nurtures and even encourages growth. By pruning, in which we trim branches that have grown upward and outward, we create an opportunity for restored growth.

The idea of cutting something back to encourage growth does not make sense to me. I would prefer to let things grow wild. Then there's no deciding when to prune and clip. No wondering which branch to snip. Why can't we just let plants do their thing?

To me, this unsupervised approach lets plants do what plants arguably do naturally. Vines creep outward and upward, toward new spaces to claim. Branches reach upward and outward to new open areas. Roots spread and deepen. Letting plants grow with benign neglect is also easier. Surely, I think, this is the way of nature and life: wildness?

Many of us find wildness attractive. We may imagine wild, untamed country where equally untamed people, usually men, live by their own rules. Wildness, in reality, is a hard life. In the wild, most energy goes for sheer survival, leaving little energy to swirl and bank into a growth that produces and reproduces.

Without a doubt, aspects of God's creation do thrive in wildness. In our human quest for control and power, we have attempted to tame creation, often to unhelpful and even devastating effect. Rerouting major waterways creates endless issues with flooding. Monocultural farming depletes the soil and even harms our own human diets, too often filled with hypercultivated things. Wildness is necessary for both life and faith.

But *taming* is different from *pruning*. The first emerges from a desire to control, the second from a desire to tend. Pruning creates space and opportunity for growth, for thriving, even for renewal. God's creation actually "prunes," in a way, on its own. Lightning sparks fires that burn and cull the landscape of dead trees and debris. Fires help certain trees, like table mountain and lodgepole pines, to reproduce, their cones releasing seeds only when the heat of a fire opens them. Cold kills vines and branches but leaves the life under the ground, even providing more energy for spring germination.

In that sense, humans didn't come up with the act of pruning; we are simply following the guidance of God's creation.

With the invention of garden shears—compact little tools that replaced knives and machetes—we can now neatly snip branches and tendrils. I've come to think of gardening shears as holy tools easily held in our human hands. My thyme plant, my oregano, the hydrangeas that have grown wildly across my front door: all these benefit from a good pruning. Some evenings, when I get home and I'm weary from a day of endless situations that have no neat resolution, I find a pair of pruning shears and get to work.

The work of pruning, however haphazard it may seem, is not. Pruning does not mean the same thing to every plant. Some plants don't need to be pruned. Their natural growth creates ways to redirect energy for growth. Some plants can be pruned almost down to the ground, to let new growth have all the room. Others need to be pruned at certain times of year so new growth and blooms don't get sheared off in our exuberance. Even when we pay attention, we can prune too much or not enough, and we must wait until the next season to correct our mistakes.

Pruning is an art and a science. Pruning is necessary. Pruning is an act of faith.

Holding garden shears, we experience something of a sacred action. God, who gently fingers the branches, vines, shoots, and buds of our lives, trims and prunes. Divine shears seek out the dead branches that need to be removed so the ones that are living can thrive. Finding the growth that we are putting all our energy into while ignoring other areas, God snips us back. God knows the seasons of growth and the seasons of pruning for rest. And we are called to participate in this sacred gardening.

The foundational truth is that we are loved deeply by God, who knows all nooks and crannies of our souls, even the parts we would rather bury under all manner of pretty décor. This love enables us, urges us, even demands that we grow in this love so we can share this godly love with others.

Growing in love, however, is not just letting plants grow wildly. True growth does not mean merely letting the parts of ourselves we like and are proud of grow wildly while ignoring the aspects of ourselves we hope will die off quietly. Healthy growth requires pruning.

What does this look like?

We all have gifts, talents, and capacities that we're proud of and that we display to the world as beautiful blooms. These are the things about us that the world affirms. We hear how creative we are, how good we are at listening, how we're so good, so efficient, so capable. Surely God has given us these gifts to share with the world—and so we do.

We give, we share, we offer, and we let those aspects of ourselves grow. Those shiny, pretty, valued-by-others parts of our souls get all the attention and a fair amount of nurturing. Sharing our gifts feels good—as it should. Sharing our gifts brings a sense of usefulness and comfort. Tending the soil of our souls, we find these gifts continuing to grow and grow and grow.

When we aren't careful, however, these appealing and useful parts of ourselves grow with abandon—and sometimes to our detriment. Our faith involves loving and serving others. Letting that love and service grow wild—always focusing on the needs of others, the way others will see us, or the way we will be valued because of these pretty parts of our souls—has a cost. Unmitigated growth is not usually helpful or entirely holy.

I think about how rewarding it feels when we do something to help others. Maybe we deliver a meal to a friend who's overwhelmed with life. Perhaps we ask, "So how are you doing, really?" and spend time truly listening. We might even be part of a work crew that helps rebuild after a disaster. My guess is in offering ourselves and our gifts in these acts of love, we feel a sense of joy and value in these acts, which is great. While love does involve sacrifice, sharing our love also has moments of joy.

But what happens when we act so that others will love us? What happens when we assist others so we can post on social media so people will see how kind and loving we are? What happens when we share love in a bid to be rewarded and noticed?

This is when God sees the wild growth and prunes.

God the pruner is very interested in fullness—lushness, even—of our *whole* selves. And one aspect of this holy pruning means keeping trimmed back the parts of our souls we consider elegant and beautiful—often the parts of ourselves the world loves. What if pruning means letting the parts of ourselves we don't like as much have some space too?

Because let's be honest: we'd rather ignore the scraggly, broken, and messy branches of our souls. We dismiss the parts of ourselves that elicit shame, the parts of ourselves that we push aside and discount, hoping they will wither and die so we can focus on the lushness of ourselves.

Love, though, doesn't ignore or push aside. God's love for us means God finds the broken, bent, or parched parts and reminds us there is indeed life there. God may even nudge back the growth of the parts of ourselves we think are pretty, gently (or sometimes not so gently) pruning those parts so that the rest of us can get some light, space, and nourishment too. God wants all the parts of our souls to thrive.

Jesus reminds us that God is a pruner. Jesus preaches, "He removes every branch in me that bears no fruit. Every branch that bears fruit he prunes to make it bear more fruit" (John 15:2).

I wonder if we've for too long understood this verse to mean that God prunes our *withering* branches so the healthy ones can continue to grow unconstrained. What if the opposite is also true: that God sometimes prunes back our gifts and gives room for the weaker parts of our selves to get some sun?

God notices the scars and wounds and broken branches in us that we've long since written off as dead. God sees these parts of ourselves not as branches that need to go but as branches that can bear important fruit if they are given space and attention.

Carl Jung called these weaker branches of the self our "shadow" side. Our shadow side is basically all the aspects of ourselves we have deemed unworthy and unattractive: our grief, our rage, the habits and beliefs we want to hide about ourselves. Jungian analyst Ann Belford Ulanov describes it this way: "On a personal level, our shadow is all we would not be, often all our parents told us was bad behavior; it is all we would improve, all we would fix and get over, move on from."

These are the qualities we deem to be dead branches. Surely, we think, nothing can grow from them. These indeed are the things we offer to God to prune: *Here, Lord, take my anger at my father for being a narcissist. Here, prune my impatience at my own imperfections. And please cut off these dead branches of loneliness that I ignore by working eighty hours a week.*

We would rather God see all our lush growth of awesomeness, all the blooms and branches that earn us accolades and affirmations. We love that lush growth, this rogue flourishing of ego.

But rogue growth that is not truly rooted in love is dead. This wanton growth is what God prefers to prune. This is not because the ways we are sharing and loving and even serving the world are bad. Not at all. God, however, realizes that when all we do is focus on what we love about ourselves—what qualities we value, and what the world appreciates—we almost always ignore what we don't like about ourselves.

God loves all parts of us, and especially the parts we have orphaned and ignored: the branches that we have deemed worthless, the places of our souls that have been discounted. God's pruning uncovers those branches that are wilting, dry, and covered up by the pretty things. God lets them have space. God even lets us see them and notice them, perhaps give them the attention God would like us to.

Pruning makes space. A constancy of growth fills so much space that we can easily ignore the parts of us that don't fit in our image of whatever we think we should be.

Those gardening shears, in their compactness, can prune all manner of wild recklessness and unhelpful growth and share an equally powerful message about our faith. We often argue, flinch, and move away from the holy gardening shears and sacred pruning hooks. The gardening shears move toward unrestrained wildness that needs to be refocused. God can be trusted with sharp things, and with us.

# 11

# Boxes: Things That Speak of *Perhaps*

PERHAPS WE WILL get that degree. Perhaps we will get a better job. Perhaps we will write a book, or have a child, or do that thing we delayed because we had a child. Perhaps we will one day be able to remember a person, a moment, a choice without tears. Perhaps we will have a day when depression doesn't color every aspect. Perhaps they will finally stop drinking. Perhaps I will finally feel safe.

*Perhaps* is a word of possibility, however marginal that possibility may be. *Perhaps* speaks of hope, sometimes well reasoned and other times as slight as the chance of winning the highest lottery payout. *Perhaps* may be those things that we can't deal with right now, so we need a way to off-load them until the time comes when we can. So we store them away, out of sight and maybe even out of mind for a while.

*Perhaps* is regret's kinder cousin. It is faith's reality.

And *perhaps* can be the questions we face in our lives, the choices and options for our future that seem filled with direction and hope and prospect … and more than a bit of fear and trepidation. As we think about changes and chances in a world filled with both, we may find that we have an uncomfortable relationship with *perhaps*.

At some point, most of us—at least those of us privileged enough to face an abundance of choices—have to figure out what to do with all life's directions and hopes and possibilities that haven't come to fruition but still might. Do we keep chasing our dreams? Do we renounce them? Do we adapt them, shrinking them into something more attainable? Or do we try to forget them entirely?

Our culture often demands decisions, end results, and closure. But faith? Faith often wanders, even stops to rest and breathe for a while. Faith waits. Faith understands that God's sense of time isn't often as speedy or as hurried as ours.

How do we hold onto ambiguity—the questions that aren't answerable right now, the wonderings of *perhaps* and *what if* and *possibly*—in a world that prefers the known? Do we embrace the unknowns, or do we end the waiting, the unknowable?

We all own things that embody aspects of *perhaps* and *what if* and *possibly*. Many of us have boxes or bins stashed under the bed, or shoved far back in a closet, or buried under the Christmas decorations in the basement, behind the baby clothes from years ago. Boxes contain the things we have no immediate use for and even forget about—the things we might find use for someday. Perhaps. We gather these things and store them neatly away in a box, out of sight, out of our daily routines, and even out of our everyday thinking. We keep them tucked away until we discover a use for them.

We may occasionally pull out our boxes and see what's in them: photographs from decades past, of people we used to be; photos of boyfriends and girlfriends and even spouses past; diaries from when the most important thing in our lives was whether or not we'd get to go to a sleepover next weekend; letters from family and friends; ceramic trinkets that once decorated shelves of our ancestors but don't fit our modern décor; a worn stuffed animal. We may find the sheet music from the piano lessons we began, but then we got a job promotion and the idea of finally playing piano fell away with increased job demands. Or there's the travel book for the trip to Spain that was canceled because of Covid and never rescheduled.

Perhaps, God suggests, we find a container of some kind. We find some place of safekeeping to hold the items from our lives that speak of *perhaps* until the appointed time.

The Hebrew people, our ancestors in faith, wandered in the space of *perhaps* for forty years. God had liberated the Hebrews, taking them from enslavement to freedom … straight into the land of ambiguity. A forty-year sojourn took them through the wilderness of *what's next.* Forty in-between years, years of ambiguity, before they reached the Promised Land.

Many of us have heard this story, recounted in the book of Exodus, so often that we receive it with a nod and a cursory glance. But think about how anxiety-producing it must have been to wander in the desert for forty years. After the initial celebration of liberation, the excitement must have worn off. The book of Exodus affirms that the people of God did lots of complaining—like we usually do when we are in places of ambiguity and *perhaps.*

About one year into this journey, the Hebrew people received instructions from God to make a box. We call it the Ark of the Covenant, but it's a box, really. In this wooden box, coated with gold, God placed the tablets of the law, also known as the Ten Commandments. Those commandments are essentially ways to love God, to love ourselves, and to love our neighbor in all the aspects of life. Those instructions safeguard our commitments in the certainty and the ambiguity, in the times of excitement and in the times of trial, in moments of clarity and in moments of perhaps.

Then the Hebrews got to haul this box around for thirty-nine more years. They carried the box of promise with them everywhere they went. We get a considerably easier task, sort of. We don't have to literally carry around an ark filled with God's promises carved in stone. We *do* carry around the opportunities to live this messy journey of faith with all its joy and missteps. We do get to carry around things from our past that we don't quite know what to do with yet.

Some of the segments of the journey of our life are sure and certain. We are excited, grounded, even affirmed in them. They have a clear beginning, middle, and ending. We might even get closure.

Others? Well, those parts are messier, even harder to hold. All the ambiguity, the maybes, the what-ifs, and the perhaps weigh on us. They are simply too heavy to carry. So God provides a box, a place, a container that gives us somewhere to store the emotions, the questions, the wonderings for a while. Our arks can hold things until one day, we wonder what perhaps we have in there.

Maybe a change of the seasons nudges us to declutter. (Spring cleaning is a very real thing!) Perhaps we are changing other seasons in our lives—moving to a new house, adding or subtracting family members, redoing a part of our home so we have to move things out and finally need to clean out that closet or basement space. Perhaps something holy just jolts us to stop whatever we are doing and wonder about that box, that container, that space that is filled with something we need to touch.

Slowly, as we open that box we haven't opened in years, we enter into the space of *perhaps*. We unpack the narratives, relationships, recollections, and lives we have lived, all contained in small things. All the color of the past flows into full view. We find the pictures from when we were thirty years younger and wearing the party dress we worked overtime for weeks to buy. There we are, standing with the person we loved so much that when the relationship ended, we couldn't look at the dress without weeping for months. Perhaps we wondered then if we would ever love again. Perhaps we can remember, without judgment, the raw awkwardness of love that hasn't been aged and scuffed, when happily-ever-after was far more realistic—perhaps—than it is now.

Perhaps we discover a few ancient relics called handwritten letters. In a world of email and text messages, the grace and permanence of letters is fading. But there they are: notes from grandparents and great-aunts and even a few friends who have died. Arcs and strokes of pens on a postcard of Masada telling of how awe-inspiring and hot Israel is from the grandmother who loved to travel. A note from a friend checking in after a surgery, written inside of a sarcastic get-well card. Art created when we were three or eight or thirteen, when the gauge of worthy and good had not taken hold, so we simply expressed emotions in outrageously honest painting and poetry.

Perhaps we find things that aren't nearly as emotionally powerful. Tangles of charging cords, pens we could never find when we needed one. Even cloth masks from the pandemic, shoved in a box when mask mandates were lifted and we resumed some semblance of normalcy. While we do keep things with deep emotional ties to our lives, we also gather utilitarian items that simply got shoved somewhere because perhaps one day, we might need them … maybe.

These boxes, these arks, hold relics of God's love for us. Love is made manifest in our lives. Love is rarely (if ever) a clean, straight line between two certain points. It is, instead, a wandering in the desert when we long for some imagined Promised Land of safety and certainty. We long for a future when risk is reduced to nil and we know exactly where we're going, one in which we certainly aren't carrying any boxes from our past to weigh us down.

And God laughs. Then God sighs, then hands us a box, a container, a holder of memories and emotions and sensations from our past.

When we get to a place of significant transition, of tangible ambiguity, God reminds us we can stop and open whatever boxes we need to open. Even in the hardest parts of our journey, when dreams and hopes feel so far away and so scary, God is with us. Love is with us. We just might need to stop and open the box—sometimes real, sometimes metaphorical—that we've been storing our stuff in. This stuff may be our hopes we'd long buried, but some spark causes us to look again. This stuff may be another chance to forgive and reconcile. This stuff may simply be a quiet memory we need to recall to remember love.

What might a spirituality of *perhaps* look like? How might it hold all the ambiguity in which we find ourselves, contain even the cautious dreams we've convinced ourselves are simply too outrageous to imagine? What parts of our stories might we need to remember to find that perhaps there is holy wisdom in them?

God gives us a legacy of arks and deep memories and small things tucked away until we're ready. In a quiet moment, wander around your soul, your space, and see what memories and emotions and wonderings have been pushed back, underneath, or behind—things that may now need to be explored and held. What feelings do they unpack? What memories can now perhaps be dusted off and seen with the wisdom of time? What moments are worth revisiting? What dreams had you almost forgotten that God has been holding onto for you until you were ready?

God is a God of certainty and also of perhaps. Faith invites us into all these possibilities. And we have plenty of holy boxes to hold all of them safely until we are ready to unpack them, explore them.

In a world that values "closure"—which, quite honestly, is less real than the Loch Ness monster—God reminds us that life is filled with moments and feelings that can't be carried with us daily. God knows too that those things are still part of our story.

None of our story, our experiences, and our lives is wasted. Holy items give us a touchstone. As we hold something, we can let it unlock memories and emotions. Faith invites us to discern which things that speak of a perhaps can now be released. Some memories don't become less because we toss them into the recycle bin. Relationships don't become less or more because you decide the picture frame a friend gave you that never fit your décor needs to be donated or regifted instead of tucked away in a box, waiting to be pulled out only when they visit. And some regrets unknot with time, when we can see that life is never perfect, simply lived, with regrets and all.

Life and faith are lived with hope, with love, with memories and dreams. Perhaps that is the wisdom we can remember.

# 12

# Portraits: Things That Speak of Melancholy

I'm drawn to the old photographs you can often find in flea markets and antique stores. Those sepia and black-and-white images of people standing, sitting, or doing the often-mundane human activities: they take a segment in time and hold it. They pause time, letting us witness a moment.

One day, while I was on a tour of a historic home just outside Lexington, the guide showed us photographs of a child and a mother. The mother was sitting on a settee with too many parlor palms around it. She held her child in her lap.

Even by the photographic standards of the day, which rarely encouraged smiles in photography, the mother did not look happy. And the child looked asleep.

"Look closer," the guide prompted us.

My friend Brad, his husband, Frank, and I leaned in. We got out our reading glasses for a sharper focus. The truth had just begun to dawn on me when the guide whispered, "The child in the photograph is dead."

Frank immediately stepped away as if the photograph emanated some negative aura. Brad and I leaned in closer, trying to see if we really could discern whether the child was dead. We couldn't, not really. But we both could see the mother's face and we could begin to decipher the story written there.

Her features were placid but taut, as if moving any small facial muscle might have shattered the tenuous emotional control she had. The crushing sadness had pulled life from every pore. Anyone who has been devastated by grief knows too well the way that sometimes even breathing seems to be too much. Sitting seems too much. The tears wept have dehydrated our souls. We wonder if we can melt into the earth and disappear from the anguish.

Who, though, would pose a dead person in a formal photograph? The Victorians, of course, that's who. The people of the Victorian era did many things with panache and creativity, but their customs around death are without equal, except for maybe the ancient Egyptians. The Egyptian culture built great pyramids, mummified things from royalty to cats, and filled tombs with all things necessary for the afterlife. They really did set the bar for elaborate death customs.

In the Victorian era, parklike cemeteries with elaborate monuments flourished. While items and remembrances of loved ones who had died have existed for centuries, the Victorians elevated the culture around death and grief. Relatives and friends braided hair from their dead loved ones to form bracelets, hair adornments, and door wreaths. These trinkets, called *memento mori* (literally, "remember, you must die"), were objects that not only memorialized the dead; they also kept the reality of death and grief visible.

With the increasing accessibility of photography, by the mid-1800s, many Victorian people began taking photographs of loved ones, particularly children, who had died.

This memorial photography wasn't really a new idea. Before photography, many people who could afford the cost would have portraits painted of loved ones who had died as a way to remember them. Before then, people made death masks, plaster casts made soon after someone's death to commemorate the person who had died, especially someone of note. Photography, as it is now, was more affordable for most people than painters or mask-makers.

These memorial photographs show loved ones posing with the deceased person in still-life settings, on sofas or settees. They show the deceased in their coffins, in beds, or baby carriages. The photographs may include the attendees of a full funeral gathering positioned around a coffin, an almost inverse image of a wedding party.

In our world of easy photography, we take photographs of our meals, a particularly stunning sunset, even a stranger wearing an outfit that impresses or scandalizes us. But we don't take photographs of dead people. The practice seems to have fallen out of favor in the 1930s and 1940s, probably as more photographs of living people, living their lives, were available.

Victorian death photography strikes many people today as macabre. We use photography in a radically different way. We use photos to memorialize the highlights: the moments when our smiles are picture-perfect, and we're composed, and we're someplace beautiful. But I think there's more going on here than simply a cultural or generational difference in photography practices. The truth is that we are not adept at memorializing our grief at all. We don't want to remember the time we thought we might never take a deep breath again. We don't want to mull over the fragility of life. We push those thoughts aside, holding them in small spaces away from public view. We leave the grief, the sadness, the melancholy for the graveyards.

As our tour guide moved us toward the next room of the house, I took one last look at the Victorian woman holding her dead child. And I wondered again: Why?

One reason, surely, was to have a visible memory of the person who died. In a world with a high child mortality rate and without the thousands of photos and videos parents today have on their phones, I understand the need to have something tangible to show to the world: yes, this beloved child of mine did exist, even for a short while. And I wondered if having photographs of a dead child kept the reality of the fullness of life present. The story of life, after all, includes death.

And I wondered: What if those Victorians were on to something? What if, at least in this area, they possessed a wisdom we have lost: that it is important to honor the melancholy parts of life—to let ourselves feel the pensiveness of grief? Melancholy is a part of the human experience.

What things in your life represent times of melancholy—eras in which you were grieving, in which you were literally at a loss? What allows melancholy to find holy space? Are there items that you can touch and hold that will unlock the sadness that's easier to ignore? Are you ready to let those melancholic things speak?

Many cultures and faiths still give grief and melancholy their holy space. In Mexico, on the Day of the Dead, friends and family members of the dead build altars adorned with photos of their loved ones, along with candy skulls, food and drink, and ornate arrangements that give form to death, grief, and sadness. Even our modern-day communities have developed space for grief. In Hawaii, paddle-outs developed among surfers in the early twentieth century. Friends and family of the deceased paddle out on their surfboards, carrying leis and the ashes of the deceased. They form a circle in the ocean, share stories, and release the ashes and leis into the ocean.

Jews observe the anniversary of the death of a loved one by observing *yahrzeit* and lighting *yizkor* candles in memory of those who have died. The Christian faith has All Souls' Day, when those who have died are remembered by name, and Ash Wednesday, on which we remember that we are dust, and to dust we shall return.

Decoration Day, a holiday that is sadly slipping into nostalgia, was a day when friends and families went to graveyards and cleaned gravestones. Before the proliferation of perpetual care cemeteries, where the paid staff of a company maintains all the graves instead of the family, this was a necessary ritual. Adults and children would gather to clean the gravestones with brushes and rags. Fingers would trace the names and the dates of birth and death.

A Civil War–era tombstone in St. Clair County, Alabama, bears the inscription "Remember us, as you pass by / as you are now, so once were we." The verses appear on various memorials from the eighteenth and nineteenth centuries. Everyone now buried, memorialized with eulogies, even remembered with death photographs, lived a life that is worth honoring.

While you might not participate in death rituals like these, and while you might not have a photograph of a loved one in a coffin or a wreath made of your grandma's hair, you might have other things that speak of melancholy. Maybe it is the urn with a loved one's ashes. Or the wedding ring from a marriage that ended in the divorce. Or the photograph of a sibling whose life choices left deep wounds.

The power of Victorian death photography is that it captures the full reality, the completeness of human existence. These photographs are of babies who took a few breaths but never saw the fullness of life. They are photographs of a dead woman surrounded by her children, who will never hear her sing lullabies to them again. These photographs are of men who will not join their family around the dinner tables anymore and tell about their days as their children fiddled with food. These photographs capture a truth we in the Western world often want to ignore: that as they are, we will one day be too.

Try as we might, we don't get to step out of the way of the reality of death. Even when we work hard to fashion funeral services that are "celebrations of life"—services that deny the place of grief, that deny the gut-wrenching and fearful truth that we will all die—we can't fully escape the sadness. Like the ashes so many Christians get marked on their foreheads on Ash Wednesday, we humans have always needed a way to make death and our mortality tangible and touchable. Those ways are rarely full of joy. They are stark and abrupt and uncomfortable.

Often like death. Often like life.

Too often, we want the items that surround us to commemorate happy and joyful events and to prompt memories that make us smile. Photographs of birthdays, weddings, graduations, and an assortment of other celebrations involving cake are framed and displayed in our homes and offices. They are the lock screens on our phones and computers. We collage them on holiday cards and social media, sharing all this joy with the world.

The things that hold our grief, the times when we wept at the fragility of love, and the memories that are raw around the edges: these we push away into crevices. We don't display those things publicly. If we have them, we tuck them away from sight. Usually we just discard them in the hope that we can forget the hard times.

I haven't yet walked into a home with photos of everyone gathered around Grandma's coffin hanging on the wall. And honestly, if I did, I'd be a bit unnerved. All of us, even those of us in ministry and counseling and the helping professions, have been conditioned *not* to commemorate moments of sadness and melancholy. It takes active work to swim upstream, to move against our cultural commitment to happiness at all costs.

God is not afraid of melancholy, that feeling that names the world we inhabit as disappointing, heartbroken, and full of regrets. God invites us to this kind of courageous faith, asking us to remember that life is filled with a landscape of experiences. We stand on mountaintops and shout for joy, and we walk through the valley of the shadow of death asking, "My God, my God, why have you forsaken me?"

While we too often yearn to forget the upsetting and upending times of our lives, holy things can remind us of melancholy. Melancholy deserves embodiment in our homes and places of worship and community spaces. Mementos on a shelf or on the wall stand as reminders that life is a mixture of feelings and events: some good, some hard, some crushing, some joyful. Victorian death photography makes us uncomfortable because it so starkly and brutally reminds us of this truth.

The memory-keepers of melancholy find a way to remind us that despondency and grief are part of the holiness of life. And they don't need to be photographs. Many things can be touchstones to the grief and sadness we all have in our souls. They unlock feelings our culture would rather we ignore or medicate away.

Yet holiness includes times of melancholy. Holiness means we treasure the fullness of human experience rather than simply the attractive parts. Holiness invites us to reach out, to touch, and to hold the things that prick our souls and encourage our tears. Keep them somewhere you can see them. Let them remind us of sorrow. Remember that as we are full of joy, full of sadness, so is life.

# 13

# Covered Bridges: Things That Speak of Meandering

GPS CHANGED MY life. That's not hyperbole. As someone lacking an innate sense of direction, I don't get lost nearly as frequently as I did in the pre-GPS days. The apps even tell me when I need to leave to arrive at the right time. Travel, even for a directionless person like me, is now remarkably efficient.

Until it's not.

One late autumn afternoon, I found myself driving in the middle of the hills and hollers of eastern Kentucky with no cell phone signal. I'd taken a trip for a church meeting, and I was heading home to Lexington. After an initial panic—realizing I couldn't access much of a map, and I certainly didn't have the automated voice telling me to turn left or right for the best route home—I realized that if I just drove westward, I would eventually end up somewhere close to home. Eventually.

I kept driving, and the paved road shifted into a dirt road—which actually didn't bother me at all, since directions to my childhood home included "Turn off the paved road." But the dirt road narrowed, and then narrowed some more, and then kept narrowing: from one where two vehicles could pass, to one that would allow for two cars to pass only if one pulled into the strip of darkening leaves piled on either side.

After a few twists and turns, one turn opened onto a road that led to a covered bridge. I stopped my car, thinking it would be prudent to inspect the bridge for recent use. Tire tracks suggested the bridge had been used recently, and perhaps even frequently.

The experience of crossing a covered bridge in a car is a modern one. Our automobiles drain covered bridges of their original meaning. Covered bridges sing of a time when walking and horses moved people from place to place more slowly and deliberately. The lack of speed meant people didn't get anywhere quickly and had more time to notice their surroundings. They could feel the weight of the air, crisp with fall and winter chills, fresh with spring's life, or heavy with summer's humidity. They could notice the world more deeply as the angles of their vision moved with ease.

I didn't have a horse handy, and although it seemed like the covered bridge had recently held cars, I decided to walk across it to assess it a bit more. As I entered the bridge, the floorboards gave slightly. The bridge was a splendid blend of tin and wood and leisureliness. The wood that filled the sides was laid in a latticework pattern, with more than a few broken segments that let the afternoon sunlight stream in, but only in parts and pieces. The interior was muted—light enough that I could see, and dark enough to give the air a weight. It felt like a dark cathedral lit only with a few candles. The interior smelled of age and forgottenness.

I stood in the middle of the bridge for awhile and listened to the river, to the acorns dropping onto the tin roof and rolling down, and to the silence.

Eventually, reluctant to leave behind this hidden holy space I'd discovered, I realized I did need to continue my journey. I got back in my car, put it in gear, and drove through the bridge. I kept driving west, toward home. Eventually I found familiar roads, and I arrived home merely an hour later than expected.

Direct routes, straight lines, and efficient courses are all excellent ways to travel, both on roadways and in our lives. We see a destination, a goal, something to accomplish, and then we plan our path, the way we will reach this point. Directness is usually a key factor.

Finding the direct route is not the only goal for finding our way in life, however, and at times, perhaps not the best way. The efficiency of direct routes, as seen by our interstate system, does get us places faster, but at a cost. We miss the side roads, the small towns with people sitting on front porches, and the places people hurrying from one meeting to the next miss. If I had not gotten lost, I would have missed out on the meandering that led to a covered bridge in rural Kentucky. I would have missed the quiet beauty of an almost-forgotten treasure. Sometimes sacred places can be found only by meandering.

Efficiency matters in our culture, and for good reason. Anyone who has stood in line waiting to renew a driver's license can appreciate the value of efficiency. Efficiency, however, is not a cardinal virtue of the faith.

Wandering, meandering, even drifting are all holy ways of movement. God seems to bake into our faith the human impulse to wander a bit. Too often our culture expects us to have a plan, a direct, clear, do-this-and-don't-do-that plan, all before we are twenty-one, as if the end goal of life is to take the most direct route to whatever Promised Land we've imagined for ourselves.

But what if the end goal of both life and faith isn't really a goal? What if the entirety of a life of faith is to wander, to notice, to listen for the voice of God speak to us in the most unexpected ways and through the most unexpected things? We can always turn around, we can backtrack, we can get lost and meander. There isn't a finish line or a position we achieve in which we have finally "won" at life or at which we have "arrived." Our journeys of faith are journeys of meandering.

Too often, faith is couched in certainty—in a goal we see ahead of us that, once accomplished, will mean we have arrived. We were lost and now we're found. We were condemned and now we're saved. We reduce faith to a straightforward movement: from the land of the damned to the place where we follow God. We think it's a direct route with no side trips or dead ends.

Except that faith is mostly about the side trips and dead ends. Faith is the wrong turns we took, where we discovered an amazing, out-of-the-way place that caused us to sit for a while and enjoy this new thing that ignited our imagination. Faith is a meandering wander into strange new lands. It's encountering people who speak differently about God than we do, causing us to retrace our steps and explore a different perspective.

I wondered how much I miss—how much we all miss—because we are more concerned with directness and efficiency. What gets lost when we forget the holy value of meandering?

The word "meander" comes from the Greek word *maiandros*: the name of a river in Caria, which was in southwest Anatolia, with a winding and twisting course. Faith is often about winding and twisting. Sometimes the things we had hoped would direct us don't work, so we twist and turn our way to another option. Sometimes the goal we sought keeps moving, so we wind our way around until we face another direction and see another way God invites us to walk.

I didn't know that a Greek name for a river gave a name to the experience of faith I had as I stood over a river in eastern Kentucky. That river was spanned by a covered bridge, tucked away into a holler. But there, on an eastern Kentucky byway, was a reminder that meandering has existed longer than efficiency.

The covered bridges that still exist are usually located off the main road and out of the way. Somehow they have avoided the fate of so many others, which were replaced by efficient replacement bridges made of iron and steel. The covered bridges that remain were simply left alone on isolated ways, spanning creeks and rivers along roadways that meander. To find one, we have to be willing to meander. To appreciate one and listen to its stories, we have to be willing to get out and walk (or ride a horse). We have to let go of our allegiance to efficiency in order to let a bridge speak.

The great practices of faith—prayer, contemplation, self-examination, and discernment—are not efficient practices. They invite us to meander on the side roads, exploring places and encountering feelings we would completely miss if we took the most direct route. Our life of faith is not one of desperately seeking the most direct route from heathenism to salvation; it means exploring the wild lands and meandering in the trust that what we encounter will expand our vision of the sacred.

The ancestors of our faith did quite a bit of literal meandering. In the Bible we find stories of people meandering in places for long periods of time. People wandered and roamed and rambled. Almost no one in our story of faith in the Bible gets from point A to point B by a direct line. A big story of wandering is the account of the Hebrews, who meandered for forty years in the wilderness, from Egypt to the Promised Land, a journey that would take most people walking in a straight line a month, at most. Forty years? That required lots of meandering.

But there are so many accounts in the Bible of people who were told to go to one place and who then wandered. Sometimes they meandered to make the journey as long as possible to avoid God, other times they were following God, and other times they were lost. Some probably meandered, well, just because.

My favorite meandering account involves a talking donkey and a deeply conflicted man named Balaam. Balaam is a great prophet solicited by the Moabites to curse the Jewish people. The story in the book of Numbers shows that even God meanders back and forth. God first tells Balaam not to go with the Moabites. Then God says to go, but orders Balaam to listen closely to God's instructions. Balaam goes, finally thinking he's set out on the right path, the most direct one. God, however, decides otherwise and sends an angel to block Balaam's way. And yes, I realize that God told Balaam to go. In this story, everyone meanders except the donkey.

Balaam is on the path he thinks he's supposed to be on, except no. His donkey can see that the angel of the Lord is blocking Balaam's way. The donkey won't go, and Balaam unhelpfully beats the donkey—who, of course, is the one character in this whole account who is actually making wise choices.

God then gives the donkey the capacity to speak, and she basically asks Balaam, "What is your problem? Maybe you should pay attention when I don't want to go forward on a path."

Balaam, who seems not at all shocked by a talking donkey, recognizes her wisdom and finally listens to God. Balaam becomes the source of a blessing for the Jewish people before they enter the Promised Land.

Yes, direct routes sometimes matter. But meandering—that plain old act of wandering, which humanity has been doing for thousands of years—reminds us of the value of stepping and marveling, of stopping and noticing. Meandering is the prayerful act of exploring, and it may include both feeling afraid when we're really lost and feeling joyful in the steps we take. It may include stumbling on unexpected things like covered bridges.

Meandering is sacramental: an outward experience of some inward grace, perception, and transformation God yearns for us to have. When I give myself time to meander, my soul can better hear the whisperings of the mystics, especially the desert mothers and fathers. Those people of faith looked at the organized church of their day, which had become too concerned with moving with efficiency. And that meandering group of people, committed to the teachings of Jesus, decided to walk away from that organized force of power. Essentially, they decided to go for a walk. They walked into the desert wilderness with no real place to go. They wandered into caves. They meandered in the wilderness like Jesus did for forty days. They recognized the holy act of being instead of accomplishing.

The writings and practices of the desert elders still invite us to contemplate what we are seeing, hearing, tasting, and feeling when we encounter God. When I meander, I am present in the moment, letting God's presence wash over me and reminding me to notice.

I take issue with J. R. R. Tolkien's oft-quoted line, "Not all who wander are lost"—or at least with how the line, from his poem from *The Fellowship of the Ring*, has come to be understood. Maybe not all who wander are lost, but a goodly number of we humans who wander *are* lost. And being lost isn't always a bad thing. Meandering in this state of lostness can be a good thing, a holy thing, and a human thing.

Being lost introduces us to things we haven't seen before and immerses us in experiences that our routines would normally prevent. Being lost allows us to be a little afraid. And feeling fear, while not necessarily a state to be lauded as a permanent state, can be the emotional equivalent of stretching our muscles, causing fibers to tear and reform in stronger and more durable ways. Being lost often involves being uncomfortable, a little on edge, a step or a mile outside our comfort zones.

What if we recognized the spiritual value of meandering? What if we committed to wandering? What if we let ourselves be surprised and delighted by the covered bridges we stumble on, the shelter we find in the unexpected places that weren't on our initial agenda? And all those places hold some holy insight for us. Meandering, literally speaking, is a way to let our external movement, even if it's just across town, to change us. Meandering, in a spiritual way, changes us too.

Our life is a series of meanderings. God links those meanderings together for us, inviting us to take the long way home. Along the way, we get glimpses of what our true home with God will look like. On this journey, God gives us permission to be lost, to wander, to not know. God speaks to us through the people and places we encounter, and God also reminds us that the wandering will form us. Each place we encounter, each experience that calls us—to take another step when the road is not clear, to be afraid or simply intrigued because we are lost—is part of faith.

# 14

## Reins: Things That Guide

WHEN I WATCH new riders at the barn, I often wonder what we humans did to deserve the patience and serenity of horses. As riders are developing their balance and strength for riding, they often pull back tightly on the reins. Reins, which are straps of leather or nylon or even plastic that attach to the bit and bridle of a horse, rest in the rider's hands. The reins allow communication to the horse's mouth and head through the movement of our hands. A slight tug back usually tells the horse to slow down or stop. A movement left or right will direct the horse in that direction.

The default action of so many beginning riders, though—and even a few riders who have spent a lot of time in the saddle, when we feel shaky—is to pull the reins to try to right themselves. But reins are actually not all that helpful when riders are half a second away from tumbling to the ground.

Sometimes I wonder what horses think about the rein-happy humans on their backs. I imagine these tried-and-true horses trotting around the arena, thinking, *Why do you keep doing that? Do you actually think this annoying force will stop me?*

Yes, a horse might stop when you pull on the reins, but that's only because they've carried enough riders to know they are learning. Horses know—and sometimes riders learn—that reins are not meant to balance. Reins are meant to guide.

Reins are part of horse tack because of their role in guiding the horse, not balancing the human in the saddle. Balance is on us—to develop strength and confidence and technique. Most horses don't enjoy riders who use their reins to balance because doing so pulls on the bit and bothers a horse's mouth.

Reins work to guide horses because they utilize the horses' immense sense of feeling and movement to communicate. Horses feel pressure and move away from it. The directing power of reins comes not from muscle and might but from feel, from touch, from recognizing a rider's preferred communication style.

Reins guide because they communicate not with shouts or demands but with subtle shifts and movements. Smallness speaks volumes to horses in part because horses are profoundly sensitive. They can sense a fly landing on one hair in their tail.

They can notice a distant movement or smell long before their rider can. Sensitivity is built into their bones. That sensitivity means small movements, small gestures, and small actions communicate very loudly to horses.

Humans, like horses, are born instinctively to notice smallness around us—subtle shifts in our environments, our feelings, and our instincts. We, like horses, are the product of millions of years of evolution. Noticing small details around us served to keep our species alive. Noticing these small things guided us to pay attention to our inner selves, to stop walking and look around, and to notice.

We humans, like horses, can be guided. We may even need to be guided. The questions that we eventually begin to ask as we pursue a spiritual life include: What—or who—guides us? How sensitive are we to the small nudges and shifts of the Spirit? How do we let God guide us?

Many of us have had the experience of someone coming to mind, realizing we haven't talked to that person in a while, and reaching out, only to discover that we've reached out at just the right time. "Thank goodness you called! I need to talk to someone," the person might say, or "How did you know to stop by right now? I could use some help," or something similar.

Or perhaps we have paid attention to that nudge that seems to come from nowhere: To apply for a job that ends up being the exact career move we needed to make. To befriend the refugee family down the street whose close friendship over the years becomes the impetus for our child to study the language of their home country in college. Or perhaps we've felt prompted to simply sit, day after day, in moments of silence—when suddenly one day, the tangled issue that has kept us wrapped and twisted inside is unknotted and we can breathe.

People frame that inner guidance system in different ways. Some call it instinct, others intuition. Others recognize this guidance as the Holy Spirit. Whatever you want to call it, I believe God guides us through these small interior movements of the soul.

God's guidance is embodied in all sorts of things that shift and nudge. Our challenge is to recognize which promptings are holy guidance. God guides us in the small movements, shifting us, reminding us God is still there, directing us.

Christians often say that when we are struggling with a big thing, we want God's guidance. But we usually want the blinding, impossible-to-miss guidance that stops us in our tracks and gives us no other option. "Why can't God talk to us like God talked to people in the Bible?" we may lament. We'd love a clear writ from the Almighty that says, "Do this and don't do this." Personally, I would love a clearly printed list of holy directions, telling me exactly what to do with all the conditions and possibilities before me. I want a sure and certain message—a hard pull in one direction on a rein that leaves me no other choice about which direction God wants me to go.

I've done that with a few horses over the course of my riding life. Sometimes, when I've given a subtle nudge with the reins and received no response, I've given a harder pull to get the horse's attention. Some horses respond to that firmness. But others? Well, let's just say stubbornness is not only a human trait.

Some horses shake their heads and use their considerable strength to continue moving in the direction they want to go. In the ongoing discussion, carried out via rein and pressure and bit, the horse and I argue about which direction to go. I add more pressure and guidance. When I ride some particularly stubborn horses, this means we go their way first and then wander around a bit before getting on the right path.

I think humans are more like horses than we want to admit. God is always guiding us, inviting us into a holy back-and-forth of instincts tugged, ideas granted, notions prompted. It's just that we like to ignore the nudges and go our own way.

We love the story of the angel appearing to Mary to clearly state she is called to be the mother of Jesus, and the story of the shepherds—which, from our point of view, leaves no doubt as to the guidance of God: they get the instructions and run to the manger in Bethlehem to see the baby Jesus.

More common in scripture, however, are the many accounts of less clear holy guidance. Many people in scripture just kind of muddle through. They hear God and do the exact opposite. They make their best guesses as to what God is telling them. Many people in scripture simply respond, react, and even manipulate or scandalize as they make small choices in their lives. Naomi's small movement in following God—placing Ruth in a particular field so that she'll be in the path of Boaz—leads to the big continuation of the line of David. And there's the story of the women who follow their intuition or holy guidance or whatever we may call it to save Moses. The Hebrew midwives Shiphrah and Puah defied Pharaoh's decree to kill all Hebrew baby boys at birth, saying the Hebrew women were vigorous and simply gave birth before they arrived. They undoubtedly helped Moses's mother, as she birthed him and secretly nursed and cared for him for three months. When he is too old to hide anymore, his mother creates a small ark and floats him in the Nile. His sister follows the tiny ark in the reeds until she sees one of Pharaoh's daughters discover Moses. When Pharaoh's daughter decides to keep the foundling Moses as her own, Moses's sister quickly ensures his biological mother will be his wet nurse. Three women and small movements ensured the great patriarch and prophet Moses would go on to make his own journey with God.

Subtle moments of guidance, from light pressure and slight movements, really can end up being the great actions of faith. God's holy reins shift subtly, applying a bit of pressure here or a touch of guidance there. And the thing about God's way of guiding us is that God's style leaves lots of space for us to be part of the guidance as well. We've still got agency. Sometimes we are clearly, forcefully guided away from a bad, harmful choice and toward a good one. But that's rare. Most of the choices we have to make include possibilities that are neither holy nor evil, neither perfectly right nor perfectly wrong. Many decisions we have to make are between one good thing and another good thing. Such decision-making is often deeply nuanced and difficult, with repercussions that aren't always celebrated.

God's reins are flexible, loose, and guiding. They nudge and suggest. God's way of steering doesn't override our will; it *involves* us. Personally, I think of that as an astonishingly questionable decision on God's behalf, given humans' track record of making bad decisions despite very clear holy guidance on basic tasks (like "don't eat the fruit of that tree").

For better or worse, God offers guidance to us in some big ways and in many small ways. And to be aware of God's guidance, we need to pay attention. We need to create space in our lives to notice, to discern, and to reflect.

This place of focus, this time of attention, is a place where we can know, truly, who we are. We can get to know our own voice, our own longings. We can learn to listen to the still, small voice within us that rejoices when we find our bliss. That way, when guidance offers us something new, some new insight, we can shift accordingly. We can be moved wherever God's reins want us to go.

Sensing God's guidance in our journeys and discerning God's movements in a life of spirituality is absolutely necessary. Prayer, community, holy writings: all are ways we are subtly and even brashly directed in our journeys. When a holy directive from God gently nudges us or affirms our current direction, we often feel a sense of calm. We may find ourselves feeling sure and secure even in the midst of a change.

And when the guidance takes us on a journey to a place that seems uncomfortable, even frightening, we might feel uncertain and anxious. We might wish God would pull the reins, hard. We often want our guidance to be show-stopping and awe-inspiring. God definitely contains the possibility of dramatic display, as we see in scripture, with burning bushes and archangels popping into a lazy afternoon to change a woman's life.

But the guidance that comes in less dramatic forms is still as truthful and just as holy. The reins of insight that nudge us to text or call a friend we haven't seen in a while. The touch on our souls when we hear a hymn that causes us to tear up, opening some emotion or memory we have ignored and need to attend to. The slight movement of anger that we usually quickly bury but that might be a holy nudge to realize something is off, or that we need to speak up about injustice that treats other children of God as if they aren't fully deserving of love.

Pay attention. Let the subtle movements of God lie against your soul and guide you. Let yourself be shifted. Be guided.

# 15

# Quilts: Things That Speak of Redemption

EARLY IN MY ministry, a friend shared a story about a friend who had just moved to the Deep South and was enamored with the beautiful quilts displayed in her mother's home. In many Southern homes, quilts are draped over the backs of sofas and spread across the foot of beds. With their colorful scraps of fabric sewn into intricate and elaborate patterns, quilts make the most of fabric that isn't enough on its own to do anything with. But piece it together? Suddenly there is a quilt.

This woman asked my friend's mother where she had bought her lovely quilts. My friend's mother, in her deeply Southern way, responded, "My dear, we don't *purchase* our quilts in the South. We *inherit* them."

As someone who has inherited at least five quilts, I identify with this woman's response. We do inherit them, these patched-together pieces of art.

Quilting is an ancient art form that blends beauty and function. Across centuries and cultures, quilters, most of whom are women, have sewn scraps of material in layers with padding (I grew up calling it batting) in between. Quilts keep people warm. Quilts add beauty to a home. Quilts also tell a story pieced together from scraps.

My great-aunts and grandmothers would take old dresses and shirts that had reached a state in which no more patching could render them wearable, and they would save them in baskets. When there were enough scraps, the women would gather and quilt.

Quilting is a communal event, from the piles of random scraps gathered from multiple sewing baskets to the sheer size of the quilting frame. Even as a child, I knew that quilting bees were functional and fun. I have memories of watching women gather, usually three or four, at my great-aunt's home. They would bring tablecloths and house dresses, baby clothes and pieces of fabric unused from another sewing project. As they were setting up, they would organize their fabrics, some already cut into precise shapes for the quilt, others waiting to be envisioned into their next life.

Aunt Teb would hold up some baby clothes, last used by her grandson who could now drive. Her neighbor Ella would smooth out an embroidered tablecloth that everyone admired until Ella pointed out the stain that didn't come out even after several rounds of laundering. Another friend would offer fabric she found at the church rummage sale with a pattern that left no doubt as to why it ended up in a church rummage sale.

Before "Reduce, Reuse, Recycle" became a slogan for environmentalism, it was a practice of artists who quilted. Things that could be seen as remnants, trash, and scraps were just in search of a new expression that used the old things.

God is a lot like Aunt Teb and her neighbor Ella and the other women who gathered at my great-aunt's house. God uses old things to fashion newness. And God does not discard scraps or broken things or even things that are past their shelf life.

Do *we,* though? Most of us live in a world very focused on the newest, the latest, the most current thing. When something is passé, out of date, a bit worn, or simply broken, we discard it.

Some things, though, can't be discarded. Or shouldn't be. The scraps of our lives, the pieces of our souls that are worn and threadbare, the parts of our stories that are stained: all are things we want to toss away as worthless, certainly too worn to be useful.

What are the things you have tossed away? What types of things do you remember that bring that flush of shame and that weight of failure? Perhaps they include a relationship that didn't live up to the expectations, a job that ended in failure, a memory that still feels tattered in your soul.

Think of the events, relationships, and memories that are not celebrated by framed photographs on the wall. Think of the things in your life that are rent by the disappointments, the wounds, and the pain.

Surely, we think, when we remember all *those* things, they are not of any value. No one wants to see them. So we throw them away. Or at least try.

Yet God always finds our scraps: the pieces and parts that don't seem to fit anywhere. God does something that God can do: recreates something of exceptional worth.

Historians and art critics, while appreciating quilting as an art, often categorized it as "folk art." Art, yes, but not at the level of Artemisia Gentileschi and Mary Cassatt.

The women of Gee's Bend, Alabama, let their work bear witness to the art of quilting. Because of its geographic isolation in a bend of the Alabama River, Gee's Bend, also known as Boykin, created an insular community for Black Alabamians. The quilters of Gee's Bend are the descendants of enslaved people and sharecroppers of the area. The Gee's Bend quilters create quilts of profound originality that break with the traditional European-American patterns for quilts. Quilts brought warmth and exquisite beauty into the homes of residents who were too often unable to afford heat or denied the capacity to buy much of anything because of racism. Beauty slipped in, as it almost always will.

The daughters and granddaughters and great-granddaughters of women who had been enslaved by white Alabamians took scraps and formed patterns, some intricate, others simple. The patterns were based on Indigenous art and images the artists noticed in the routines of their lives over the decades and centuries. The quilts made by the women of Gee's Bend are a harmony of beauty and functionality. Today, those quilts still warm beds, still get passed from one generation to another, and now hang in some of the great museums in our country, a symbol of functionality and beauty. Scraps made into something of great value.

Holiness, like quilts, is almost always a blend of functionality and beauty rendered from scraps and refashioned into something different. Life leaves us with scraps, those pieces of our selves that have been so used and so worn by the work of living that we are certain they aren't worth keeping. We toss them away, these remnants of emotions, memories, and choices we wish we hadn't made. Surely, we say to God, these are beyond any use.

Yet God finds unexpected ways of taking the scraps of our lives, our attention, even our selves, and patterning them into something more, even something beautiful. Scraps in the hands of God are never oddments or things to be discarded. They are, in fact, the very source of useful beauty.

Quilters know that quilting means waiting until there are enough scraps. Sometimes they add larger purchased pieces of fabric, but the heart of quilts is the parts and pieces that come together over time to be formed into something whole and new and needed. Quilters salvage the ragged and the torn things, and in a mighty act of creativity, they render them into something else entirely.

We call this redemption, which might be one of God's most astounding powers.

Redemption is the miracle that takes the shreds and pieces of life that we humans tear asunder and transforms them into something valuable, useful, and worthwhile. In the book of Genesis, the saga of Joseph and his brothers is filled with redemption.

Joseph is, we learn as we read, his father's favorite, which means he is, quite honestly, a rather arrogant little brat. He gleefully tells his brothers of dreams he has in which they bow down to him. Dad gives Favorite Son a coat of many colors, which he parades around in while telling his brothers how great he is.

It is not hard to see why his brothers had had enough of him, is it?

Still, they respond with appalling force. They shred the coat of many colors and tell their father that Joseph is dead.

Joseph, however, is not dead. Thanks to the mercy of his brother Reuben, he has instead been sold to passing merchants. Joseph finds himself enslaved in Egypt. We can presume he is sitting in the shreds of the pieces of his life. We can also presume he has learned some valuable and beautiful skills, like humility.

Time marches on, as it does. Stitching together the scraps we humans tear apart takes God some time. Eventually Joseph, who has become a man of great authority in Egypt, is reunited with his brothers. After playing some mind games on them—because Joseph is still human and probably needs to rend his brothers' lives asunder for good measure—the family is reunited. In a stunning scene of recognition, forgiveness, and redemption, Joseph says to his brothers, "What you meant for evil, God meant for good" (Genesis 50:20).

While the story doesn't say it, I like to think Joseph's coat appeared in the story at that moment when he was reunited with his father and brothers. I like to imagine that, after the tears and hugs and moments when no one could speak because their emotions were just so much, Joseph's father may have opened his bag and pulled out the coat of many colors. Maybe it had been resewn together, or perhaps it was still ripped. The coat of many colors was certainly now too small for an adult man to wear. But the story of redemption—its plot and arc and theme embedded in the scraps—still fit. Maybe Joseph refashioned it for his nephews or his own children to wear. Maybe he just kept it as it is.

We can often forget that sometimes the scraps tell their own story of survival. Joseph's life, his father's and brothers' lives, and our lives: all are quilted together by God's gifts of time, confession, forgiveness, and love. What we wear out, God refashions. What we rip, God redeems. What we tear, God mends.

We all have scraps and pieces and parts that have been deeply worn and torn by suffering and crisis and catastrophe. We can unhelpfully frame these events in life as God's doing. Some theologies say God does the breaking, the tearing apart, so that God's glory is somehow revealed. I disagree. God allows life to happen, yes, and life means tearing and mending, sowing and reaping, and wounding and healing. But God doesn't have to get involved for things to rip and break. We humans do a fine job of breaking each other and ourselves, which no doubt shatters God's heart.

Instead of forever cushioning us from the consequences of personal and community choices with which we wound each other, God imbues creation with the wisdom of quilting. We aren't all that adept at piecing and reforming. For that, we need God's quilting prowess. We need God to remind us that no part of our selves and souls is beyond redemption, beyond being useful in another way. Mistakes are pieced together with threads of God's compassion. Personas we wore when we were younger but no longer fit can be altered. God's love provides the framework to sew all these parts and pieces into something renewed, refashioned, and redeemed.

God treasures the things we throw away or stop caring about. God adores these scraps of our selves. God longs for us to sit in the holy space long enough to see the quilt that God creates from what we thought were worthless scraps. God touches those scraps like women over centuries. God fingers them, noting the beauty of small patterns. God reshapes our scraps into new things, useful things, even extraordinarily beautiful things.

# CONCLUSION

MANY SOUVENIRS REMIND us of a rush of joy, of levity, of adventure. We all have some of these, I imagine: objects from our lives that affirm us and the stories we tell ourselves, that bring smiles when we remember them. The diplomas we earned, the trophies proclaiming a victory, the trinkets from vacations and escapades: these serve as touchpoints for good moments. Joy exists, these souvenirs remind us—and joy needs to be shielded and remembered. They are holy things, these tangible objects, that allow us to connect with delight, joy, and accomplishment. Life is hard enough, and we need reminders that we are flourishing.

Our souls need souvenirs of our holy journeys.

Life is joyful, and life is challenging and arduous. Perhaps the souvenirs that are most holy, most helpful to our faith journeys, are the ones that remind us we are messy and grieving survivors. These objects pull us into moments that are bittersweet, even uncomfortable to remember. They are ordained to keep memories, feelings, and storylines that we might rather tuck away in boxes, hoping, perhaps, we'll forget.

But forgetting has a cost. We humans can forget, for so many reasons. Sometimes we need to off-load some memories and stories until some later date when we are able to pick them up again without the weight crushing us. Sometimes we ignore the uncomfortable memories, and these relics guard the gateway to the deep stuff of life and faith, the moments and memories we might otherwise conveniently forget. These souvenirs are keepers of the memories we don't really want to share, sometimes because we are not the hero of these stories. Sometimes they even serve as touchstones for God's invitation to grow in some dimension of our spiritual life.

Our lives are filled with souvenirs of the holy. I've shared some of the things present in my life that hold memories, wisdom, and prayer. They are things, and they are also more than things. They are touchpoints to God, and they are found everywhere in our lives. We just need to look.

Jesus tells us to seek and we will find (Matthew 7:7). What objects do you seek or, more accurately, perhaps just stumble upon? And what aspect of faith, of holiness, of God do you find?

Sometimes we find holy objects when we are cleaning out a drawer. Perhaps we dump the contents out on a bed simply because it's time to declutter … and there it is: the thing. Perhaps we pick up the thing and remember something that we've pushed away, pushed back, and hidden. Maybe, we think, if we edit enough, we can erase all of that, all of the tattered parts of our lives.

And yet there it is. The key to the home you shared with a partner until the idea of being together was suffocating and "until death do us part" evaporated into a promise you knew you had to break. The candle marking the birthday that started a year that you still wonder how you survived. The photo of a relative who died, a loved one who harmed you, and your first thought is, *I thought I threw all of these away.*

When we ask God what the things that are important to us can reveal, we might find a memory that slides under our skin, one we had almost forgotten. We might find a dream we had pushed aside. We might hold an experience of God that we hadn't considered before.

All these souvenirs—the ones that bring us joy and the ones that catch us in melancholy—are the holy stuff of faith. Our lives are filled with ways to touch God in a very real way. Holy things surround us in our homes, our places of work, in all places where we live and move and have our being.

You have now read about fifteen things in my life that serve as souvenirs of the holy. Hopefully those things have helped you glimpse the things in your life that connect you to God. If you haven't done so yet, take a moment (or several).

Look at the things that you have sitting on shelves around your house, hanging on the wall, stuck in the backs of drawers, or growing outside. Notice them. Hold them. Feel God in them.

The next section of this book offers some prayers you may use to deepen your encounter with God through these things. We can create rituals and prayers around the things we hold sacred in our lives.

Let these souvenirs remind you of the messy, joyful, muddled, and hopeful moments that make up our lives of faith. Let these things speak to you about God. Let these items tell your holy story.

# PRAYING AND MEDITATING WITH YOUR SOUVENIRS OF THE HOLY

HERE ARE FOUR moments of prayer to use by yourself or with a small group as you contemplate and reflect on the objects that hold holy meaning for you. These object prayers can be used as part of a regular prayer practice, as you're cleaning out a drawer, closet, or attic space. Or you can use them as a way to let your spiritual imagination wander into new insights about the things that share space with you. They can be used however you like: out of order, over the course of a week or season, or in a moment, by yourself or with a group. They are simply tools to let the objects that surround you speak of God's presence, love, and wisdom in your life.

## Praying with Ordinary Things

*Almighty God, who creates all that is and gives us all that we possess: I thank you for the objects of our daily life. Grant that I may see in them your holiness, often present in the ordinary and common. Allow me to treasure the things that I forget to notice because they are so present in my daily life. Give me the grace to appreciate them, to see them, to treasure them. Amen.*

What are the ordinary things in your daily life that you often overlook? Sitting in a quiet place in your home, office, or even outside, let your gaze wander, noticing a few items. Slowly allow your attention to rest on one. What task or chore does it help you accomplish? How does it help you in your daily life? What challenges would appear without this item?

Turning your thoughts toward your faith, what parts of your faith are easy to overlook? Perhaps it's a prayer you've said over and over or a hymn you've heard so many times you don't pay attention to the words anymore. Maybe it's a routine like seeing the candles lit before worship. How might the object you're seeing now remind you of the value of the ordinary and routine in your faith? How does ordinariness help you experience God? How might you offer gratitude for this object?

## Meditating on Storied Things

*God of The Word, you tell me the stories of your love. Grant that I may allow the things that surround me to tell me the stories of your presence in my life. Give me the stillness to hear the words of memories, of experiences, of moments recalled and retold. May I hold these stories and let them enlighten my faith, deepen my love, and stir my imagination as I journey in faith. Amen.*

Many objects in our lives are infused with meaning. They are relics, touchstones, and items that remind us of the people we know, the places we've seen, and the love we've experienced. All these are mementos of the ways we've encountered God in our lives. Is there an object you have that holds a particular story that prompts emotion: joy, grief, pensiveness, perhaps? Close your eyes and recall as much of the story as you can. What details emerge? What feels familiar? What surprises you? Perhaps you can share the story with someone, write it down in a journal, or record it using a voice memo app.

Take a few moments to reflect on the object and the story it holds. Where do you experience God in this story? How has your understanding of the story changed through your life? Is there a story from the Bible, from the lives of the saints, or another traditionally religious narrative that is similar? How does the object represent sacredness to you?

## Contemplating the Mystery Behind Things

*God of mystery, whose thoughts are not my thoughts and whose ways are not my ways, bring me into the places of mystery, of things not easily known, and of questions not casually answered. In this space, allow me to feel the certainty of faith while seeking understanding of those things that are confusing, hazy, and unclear. Let me wander with my thoughts and feelings to a deeper insight of your love. Amen.*

The church has long defined sacraments as outward and visible signs of inward and spiritual grace. Or, in a more basic understanding, the one way we can know what an orange tastes like is to bite into it and taste it. God is at times a deep mystery who sometimes simply cannot be explained; God is instead experienced.

That's likely why people of faith have used things to touch the mysterious. Holding a lighted candle during a Christmas Eve service to touch the mystery of the Incarnation, using bread and wine to enter into the mystery of Christ's love for us, and even holding a simple wooden cross as we pray to touch the great mystery of prayer—all are ways we use things to hold mystery as we contemplate it, question it, and explore it.

One way we allow objects to hold mystery is that we aren't always sure why we kept something. We likely all have things in our homes we're not sure why they are there, why we've kept them after all this time. Can you find one of those objects? What's its story? Where did it come from? Where do you keep it? When was the last time you thought about it? Let the object share its story with you as you wonder.

Now wonder why you keep it. Habit, perhaps. Maybe you forgot you had it. Maybe you aren't sure. The point of this practice is not necessarily to find an answer, but instead to contemplate, a Christian practice that uses silence and imagination to recognize God's presence, not necessarily to seek clarity or certainty. What does this object say about God through its presence in your space and in your life? What does this object invite you to experience about mystery?

## Releasing Things

*God of lost sheep and found coins, thank you for giving me this item to have, to hold, and to use for a time. Give me grace to let go of memories, emotions, thoughts, and things that have served their holy purpose with this object, that I may surrender this from my life. Be with me in my doubts and uncertainties that may accompany this moment. Remind me of your truth that in releasing, we are also making ourselves ready to receive. Amen.*

The writer of the book of Ecclesiastes states that for every time there is a season and a time for every matter under heaven. There is a time to keep and a time to throw away (Ecclesiastes 3:6b). For all the wisdom and insight things can hold for us, we all will likely encounter things that represent something of our story that can be released to God. Often, we want to keep an item because it represents a time past, a person, a moment that we revisit. And sometimes, that moment, that person, that memory no longer brings grace and understanding from our past stories and lives. We have, perhaps, learned what we needed to learn, and the object can be an unhelpful reminder that only draws us back into a time that opens wounds God is longing to heal—a wedding ring from a marriage that ended, a photograph of a parent who long ago ceased to bring love into your life, even an outfit that you wore that hasn't fit in years because bodies change with life.

Letting go is hard. We question ourselves—what if I need it someday? What if I regret discarding it? What if someone in my family might want it? Good questions, no doubt.

There is indeed a time to keep things with powerful memories. And there is a time to throw them away (or donate them or sell them—whatever feels best) because our keeping them is mostly holding on to a past that is keeping us from moving into a future God wants for us.

How do you know when that time has arrived? I'm not sure there's a clear test. Perhaps sitting with the object in some quiet and letting the memories it holds reveal themselves. What emotions stir? Are they strong and powerful? Do they feel like emotions you are watching from a distance? Maybe there are simply the residue of memories and the emotions that once accompanied them. Does the item feel too heavy for your soul to hold anymore? Or does it not feel like anything at all?

When you are ready, give thanks for the part of your life, your story, your memories, and your emotions that the object held. Then throw it away or discard it in a manner that feels appropriate. One option is also to give it to a friend to hold for a while and see if you truly feel its absence if immediately discarding it seems too hard. Remember that memories don't go anywhere—they remain yours and will continue to shape and illumine your life, even if the object that held them is gone.

# ACKNOWLEDGMENTS

THANK YOU FOR the love of deep, abiding friendships, especially my Wingswept Farm family, who are too numerous to name, and Elise, Brad, and Brian.

Thank you for the love that is St. Michael's Episcopal Church in Lexington, Kentucky. They create a community that inspires me with their love, laughter, and joy. They humble me with their capacity to sit with the broken and cherish all of our human experiences.

I have such gratitude for Nina and Murphy, my horses, who show me how much holy love is communicated through silence, presence, and the perfect smell of horses.

To those of you who read my books and share how you connect with the words, who share your stories and your loves: thank you. Writing is lonely work, and your emails, messages, and notes remind me I am not nearly as alone in this vocation as I think I am.

For Valerie, my editor at Broadleaf Books, who did exactly what editors do: love the words enough to push me to make them all count and matter.

And for Steve. I love you. You are my "I will."

Of all the things, love is the best thing. Embrace it. Share it. Rejoice in it.

# NOTES

## Chapter 1: Bread Crumbs

12 ***"The skins of onions, green tops from leeks"***: Tamar Adler, *An Everlasting Meal: Cooking with Economy and Grace* (New York: Scribner, 2011), 57.

13 ***"O merciful Lord, trusting in our own righteousness"***: Episcopal Church, *The Book of Common Prayer and Administration of the Sacraments and Other Rites and Ceremonies of the Church: Together with the Psalter or Psalms of David According to the Use of the Episcopal Church* (New York: Church Hymnal Corporation, 1979), 337.

## Chapter 4: Scars

56 ***"My scars* are *beautiful"***: Tracy E. Tyner et al., "'My Body, My Choice': A Qualitative Study of Women's Mastectomy with Flat Closure Experiences," *Body Image* vol. 46, September 2023: 419–433. www.sciencedirect.com/science/article/abs/pii/S1740144523001067#:~:text=Most%20women%20choosing%20flat%20closure,surgical%20options%2C%20particularly%20flat%20closure.

## Chapter 5: Sidelines

67 ***"How to be idle and blessed"***: Mary Oliver, "The Summer Day," in *Devotions: The Selected Poems of Mary Oliver* (New York: Penguin Press, 2017), 316.

## Chapter 9: Rocks

115 ***"The Anishinaabe understanding of land and of stones"***: Patty Krawec, *Becoming Kin: An Indigenous Call to Unforgetting the Past and Reimagining Our Future* (Minneapolis, MN: Broadleaf Books, 2022), 123.

117 ***"Being inanimate does not preclude something"***: Krawec, *Becoming Kin*, 124.

119 ***"What if the land is a being in its own right?"***: Krawec, *Becoming Kin*, 126.

## Chapter 10: Garden Shears

128 ***"Our shadow is all we would not be"***: Ann Belford Ulanov, "Where to Put the Bad? Where to Put the Feminine?" in *The Living God and Our Living Psyche: What Christians Can Learn from Carl Jung*, Ann Belford Ulanov and Alvin Dueck (Grand Rapids, MI: William B. Eerdmans, 2008), 55.

## Chapter 15: Quilts

177 ***"Quilts made by the women of Gee's Bend"***: For more on the quilts of Gee's Bend, see "Gee's Bend Quiltmakers," Souls Grown Deep, https://www.soulsgrowndeep.org/gees-bend-quiltmakers, accessed November 11, 2024.